MODEL AIRCRAFT TIPS AND TECHNIQUES
An Illustrated Guide

Mike Ashey

KALMBACH
BOOKS

DEDICATION:
FOR MY BROTHERS, ROBERT AND STEPHEN, AND MY SISTER, KAREN

Printed in the United States of America

97 98 99 00 01 02 03 04 05   9 8 7 6 5 4 3 2 1

For more information, visit our website at http://www.kalmbach.com

Publisher's Cataloging-in-Publication
(Prepared by Quality Books, Inc.)

Ashey, Mike.
   Model aircraft tips & techniques : an illustrated guide / Mike
Ashey. — 1st ed.
   p. cm.
   ISBN: 0-89024-266-6

   1. Airplanes—Models—Designs and construction.   I. Title.
II. Title: Model aircraft tips and techniques

TL770.A69 1997   629.133'1
                                   QBI97-719

Book design: Sabine Beaupré
Cover design: Kristi Ludwig

ACKNOWLEDGMENTS: Many people have helped me over the years and in many ways, directly and indirectly, contributed to this book. Thanks are due to Dr. Mia Anderson of Bergen Community College, Paramus, New Jersey; Dr. Ray McAllister, Professor Emeritus of Ocean Engineering, Florida Atlantic University; The Hobby Caboose of Tallahassee, Florida, and the Big Bend Scale Modelers Club; Glenn Johnson for his photography work; Scott Weller, Richard Boutin, Sr., and Bill Teehan of Tallahassee, Florida; Major Billy Crisler, USAF and John Ficklen of St. George Island, Florida, for allowing me to showcase their models in this book; Terry Spohn of Kalmbach Publishing; Joel and Marian Swanson for their encouragement; my parents, Joseph and Marie, for instilling within me an engine that knows no rest; and, most importantly, special thanks are due to my sons, Thomas and Gregory, for giving Dad some space to get the book done, and my wife, Kelly, for helping me every step of the way.

All color photos are by Glenn Johnson of Glenn Johnson Photoillustration of Tallahassee, Florida. All black and white photos are by the author unless otherwise noted.

CONTENTS

PREFACE

It somehow seems fitting that my two sons have included themselves in the author's photo, just as they have inserted themselves into nearly every other aspect of my life. They already have model boxes stacked in their bedroom to rival my own collection. World War II aircraft dangle from the ceiling, and the floor is sometimes littered with broken parts and pieces from both built and unbuilt kits. Our youngest son spies jets in the sky and identifies them—appropriate for our house—as "plane parts." At their ages, my sons of course emulate my interests, if not my every move. Like any proud parent I am thrilled to see them interested in the hobby that I enjoy; knowing, of course, that they will grow up to be modelers of great skill. I wonder, however, if this hobby I loved in my youth can compete with the computer and video games and entertainment packages that are available for today's youth.

So much has changed since I began working on my first book, *Detailing Scale Model Aircraft*, in 1989. I began that book because I saw a need for a basic how-to detailing book that could help any skill level modeler, from youth to adult, build better models by using common tools and materials and without breaking their bank account. I have been an avid modeler for most of my life and have watched the changes in the industry with interest, concern, and fascination. There has been a phenomenal growth in the scope of the industry, from the 98 cent Aurora, Hawk, and Monogram kits of the fifties and sixties, to an awesome array of ships, aircraft, figurines, spacecraft, and armor available in mediums ranging from plastic to metal to resin. Hand in hand with this growth has been an explosion in after-market accessories to provide details and realism in every possible fashion far beyond anyone's wildest expectation. Now your basic 98-cent model sells for 15 dollars and can be accessorized and enhanced to the cost of double, if not triple, the purchase price of the basic kit.

While this is of no major concern to the graying baby-boomer generation that grew up modeling, there is an entire generation of youngsters who are being priced out of the hobby. The next generation is the future of the scale modeling industry, and the industry is shortsighted to focus too exclusively on high-end market items. Can scale models that require creative thinking, imagination, fine motor hand coordination, and self-discipline to build compete with no-effort-required entertainment handed out by computers and video games? I cannot answer the question, but I know that unless the industry actively seeks out and encourages young modelers, it is surely doomed.

My sons may or may not pursue the hobby I enjoy, but they will have had the opportunity to try it because I have made the effort and found the time and patience to encourage them. However, there is a great need to have products available for the next generation at reasonable prices now. Every participant in this hobby, from manufacturers, after-market cottage industries, tools and accessory suppliers, publishers, and the hobbyists themselves, should encourage and support the production of models geared toward our children. The limited kits available as large scale snap tight kits from companies like AMT/ERTL, Lindberg, and Monogram/Revell are a good start, but the industry as a whole needs to do much more. I have many wonderful childhood memories starting with the first model my dad and I built together and floated in our backyard pool. I hope someday my own sons will look back fondly on their youth and remember their dad and models when they sit down with their own children, and together build my grandchild's first model.

SCRATCHBUILDING COCKPITS AND INTERIOR PARTS

There are three easy ways to make interior parts such as wing gun boxes, bulkhead framing, cockpit firewalls and consoles, and the interior areas of wheel wells. The method you use depends on the cost of the model and what part you want to make. If you are making interior bulkhead parts or framing for the fuselage you can use a contour gauge to determine the cross-sectional shape of the fuselage at a particular location, draw the part onto sheet plastic, rough-cut the part, and then form-fit the part into place. While the contour gauge will get you fairly close to the interior shape of the fuselage, it is not a precise instrument and you may have to repeat this procedure several times until you

get the hang of it. The one drawback to using a contour gauge is that the resulting shape will be for only half the fuselage. You have to be very careful about how you set up the gauge and also how you set up the drawing on the plastic sheeting so that you get the complete cross-sectional shape of the fuselage.

Another method for getting the cross-sectional shape of a fuselage or wing is to use resin to fill in the interior area, then remove it and cut it up into the cross-sectional parts that you need. This technique also works well for just about any part, especially the cross-sectional shapes of wings. You can then cut up the casting and use the resin parts as templates to draw the outlines onto

plastic sheeting. The trick with using resin is to use a mold release agent and to be sure all the seams and openings are sealed so the resin will not leak out. Pam cooking oil spray makes a great mold release agent. A very light coat is all you need. Do not use resin mold release agents that are designed to be used with RTV rubber molds, as they may attack plastic and possibly ruin it. To confine the resin to the area that you want to mold, use fresh, soft modeling clay. This works great for the interior areas of fuselages where large volumes of resin would be necessary if you tried to fill the entire fuselage. The last step is to seal all the openings with masking tape. To reduce the amount of heat generated by the resin as it is drying, pour in small quantities at a time, and let the resin cool before the next application.

Finally, a third method is to use two kits. The second kit is a sacrifice kit that gets cut up to produce the cross-sectional shape. This method works well for either wings or fuselages. The first step is to glue the halves together and then draw the cut lines on the part. These cut lines will become the cross-sectional shapes at the particular locations that you want. Once you have the locations identified, run labeling tape along the edge of the cut line and either cut the plastic with a razor saw or use a combination of a plastic scribing tool and a razor saw. I recommend making two or three passes with the scribing tool first and then finishing off the cutting with the razor saw. The labeling tape will act as a guide for the scribing tool and the scribed line will act as a guide for the razor saw. You only get one shot at this, so as the carpenter says, measure twice and cut once! Once the cut is complete, carefully smooth the surface. Now you are ready for the last step, which is to transfer the cross-sectional shape to plastic sheet stock. To do this run a grease pencil along the face of the plastic and then carefully press the opening onto the plastic sheeting. Be very careful that you do not change the shape of the cross section by holding the part too tightly, and be sure that the imprint is the same thickness as the cut surface. Another way to get the correct shape is to simply draw the outline of the outer surface of the cross section onto the sheet plastic using a .5 mm lead pencil with a sharp tip. Next, determine the thickness of the plastic, and compensate for this thickness on the cross-sectional drawing by measuring along the outer line. Use French curves to draw an identical cross-sectional shape inside the outer line. Since this is an iterative process, it may take two or three tries to get it right.

The last step is to cut the part along the inside of the imprint line. I recommend that you rough-cut the part, test-fit it, and then form-fit the part into place. To help secure the cross-sectional shape in place inside the fuselage or wing, run a tiny strip length of Evergreen strip stock along the interior area. The cross-sectional shapes will sit against the edge of the strip stock. You do not have to glue strips to both sides of the fuselage or wing, but gluing strips on both sides does help secure the part in place. To help set the strip stock in place, position a length of labeling tape along the edge of the area. It will act as a guide when you glue the strip stock in place.

Scratchbuilding cockpits is easy if you have a small supply of Evergreen strip, rod and sheet stock, a fair selection of brass rod sizes, some good reference material, and photos. Also, it is important to keep in mind that absolute accuracy is not practical or possible when you are working in scales such as 1/32, 1/48, or 1/72. What is important is a perception of scale and the size and spatial relationship between all the parts that you want to scratchbuild. In other words, appropriate sizes and shapes are more than sufficient, and the relationship and position of these sizes and shapes within such a confined area as a cockpit are what is important.

All the different shapes that you may need can be made by layering or stacking various size plastic sheet or strip stock and gluing them with super glue to achieve the thickness and sizes that you need. It is also easier to cut, sand, and shape a part to size than it is to try to stack or layer precut parts together in the hopes of getting a perfect shape. Sometimes you may have to make a part more than once to get it to look right. As long as you keep in mind that you may not get it right the first time, your scratchbuilding efforts will go a lot smoother. I have also found that using pieces of the kit parts can help

you when scratchbuilding interior components. In some instances you can get away with just modifying some of the kit-supplied parts, which will save you some scratchbuilding time. There are also several tools that are essential to scratchbuilding. One of these is a Waldron Products punch tool set. This tool is great for making consoles, but it also has a thousand and one uses in scratchbuilding, such as producing various size disks, curves, hinges, and holes. Other essential tools include an X-acto razor saw and miter box, a Northline true chopper, which will help you make clean straight cuts and reproduce multiple parts of the same size and shape, and a Northline true sander, which will help you make sure edges and sides are at perfect angles. The Northline products were originally designed for HO scale model railroad scratchbuilding, but they also work great for scale aircraft modeling.

Using accessories such as Waldron Products console instruments and placards, Reheat Models instrument decals and interior brass photoetched detail accessories, Eduard Company's photoetched interior detail sets, or Model Technologies photoetched accessories, just to name a few, will also help to achieve a more realistic looking interior, and these accessories will also save you a lot of scratchbuilding time. Last but not least, creativity and imagination play a key role in scratchbuilding and the only way to get good at scratchbuilding is to just do it!! Actually, once you jump into the world of scratchbuilding, you will get bolder and bolder in your endeavors. A final note to this discussion of scratchbuilding interior parts and cockpits: do not forget to pay attention to achieving a perception of depth and highlighting detail by using different shades of the same color paint in combination with some weathering and drybrushing when you paint all your scratchbuilt parts.

Fig. 1-1. The first step in creating an interior part using a contour gauge is to remove any interior details such as aligning pins. Here the interior section of Revell's F4F has been cleaned up and the plastic has been sanded smooth.

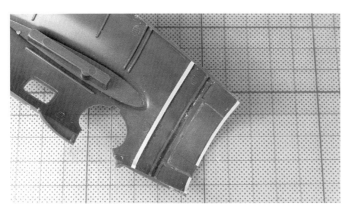

Fig. 1-3. Next use the labeling tape as a guide to glue a small section of Evergreen strip stock into place. This strip stock will act as a lip guide for the contour gauge as well as a positioning tab for the interior part.

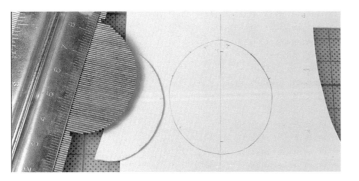

Fig. 1-5. Once you are satisfied that the contour gauge has the shape of the interior, remove the gauge and transfer the shape to sheet stock. Be sure to strike a straight line on your sheet stock so that you can use the line to position the top edge of the contour gauge. The resulting shape will appear to be a stepped curve and you will need to carefully smooth the steps into a curve. Cut out this half shape and then use it as a pattern to reproduce the full interior section.

Fig. 1-2. The next step is to position a section of labeling tape along the interior of the fuselage where you want to make the part.

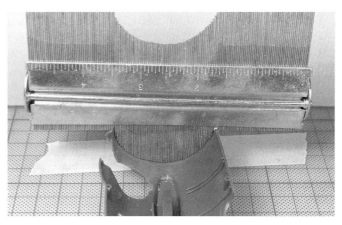

Fig. 1-4. A contour gauge is a good instrument to use to determine the interior contours of fuselage halves. Set the edge of the contour gauge against the lip of the Evergreen strip stock and slowly push the individual rods of the contour gauge down until they touch the surface of the fuselage.

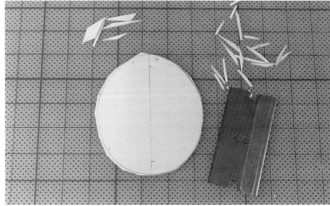

Fig. 1-6. Cut out the full interior shape using a single-edge razor blade, making tangential cuts along the edge of the shape. Form-fit the part into place and use a Flex-I-File sanding stick to adjust and smooth the edges. The contour gauge will get you close, and minor adjustments to the curve of the part should be all that are needed.

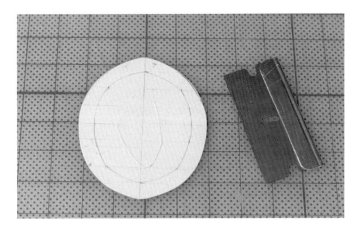

Fig. 1-7. If the part is going to become an interior frame, draw a parallel interior circle to make the part into a ring. Cut the part out, again using a single-edge razor blade, and smooth the edges.

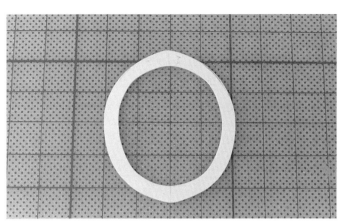

Fig. 1-8. This interior frame is now ready to be installed inside the fuselage.

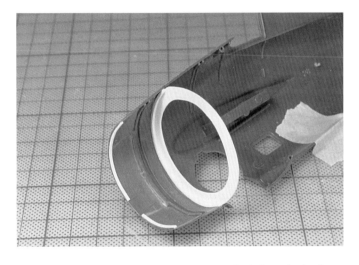

Fig. 1-9. Here the interior part has been installed along the back side of the lip of the strip stock so that the strip stock will be hidden from view.

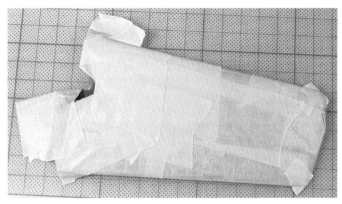

Fig. 1-10. Filling the interior area of a wing with resin is a better way to get the interior cross section of these types of parts. The first step is to clean the mating edges of the wing halves, spray the interior with Pam cooking oil spray, and then tape the halves together. You also need to completely seal the edges and any openings. Scotch 3M painter's masking tape works great for this.

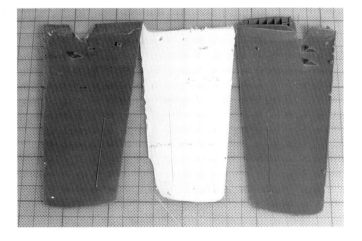

Fig. 1-11. After the resin has cooled, remove the tape and separate the part halves. You may have to use a no. 11 X-acto blade to help pry the halves apart. Here the wing halves have been separated, displaying an exact duplicate of the interior area of the wing.

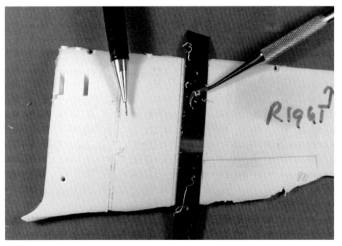

Fig. 1-12. Mark the locations where you want to cut the casting in half to create a cross-sectional shape. Use labeling tape to set the lines, and then scribe a trench using your plastic scriber.

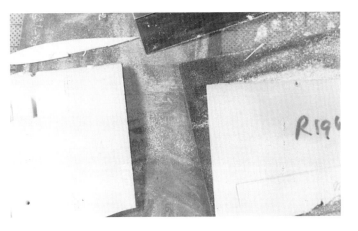

Fig. 1-13. To cut the resin casting in half use a razor saw. The trench that you scribed with the plastic scriber will act as a guide for the razor saw. After the part is cut in half, carefully run the cut surfaces across a stationary piece of sandpaper to smooth them out.

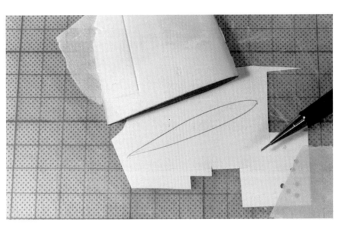

Fig. 1-14. To trace the cross-sectional shape, tape a piece of sheet stock to your cutting board. Position the cut part onto the sheet stock and carefully trace along the edge using a .5 mm or smaller lead pencil. Be very careful not to move the part while you are tracing it.

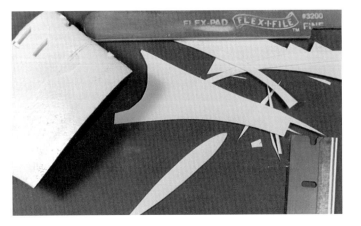

Fig. 1-15. Rough-cut the shape, make tangential cuts along the edge of the line using a single-edge razor blade, and then smooth the surface with a Flex-I-File sanding stick.

Fig. 1-16. Another technique for determining the interior shapes of wings is to use a second kit. The wings are glued together and cut lines are drawn onto the surface at the locations where interior parts need to be made. Then the wing is cut along those lines. To transfer the shapes to sheet stock, run a grease pencil along the edges of the cut-up parts and then press the edges onto the sheet stock.

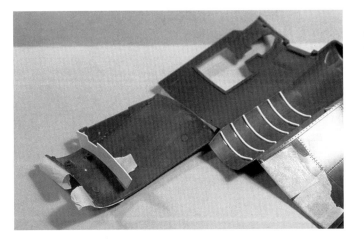

Fig. 1-17. To construct complex-looking interiors like the landing gear wells for an F4U Corsair you need to measure, cut, and form-fit the interior parts one at a time. Here the first interior section is being form-fit into place.

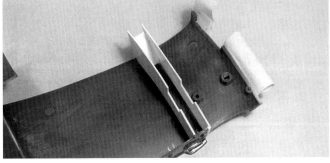

Fig. 1-18. The next step is to start to build up the interior box areas, being careful to cut, shape, and form-fit the parts into place.

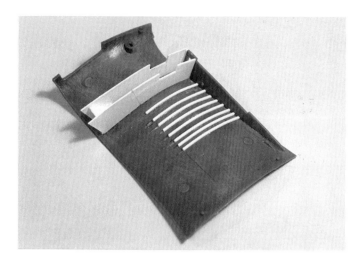

Fig. 1-19. The ribbing on the underside of the wing is easier to install before completing the boxed-in area. Note that the strips were glued in place and then cut to length.

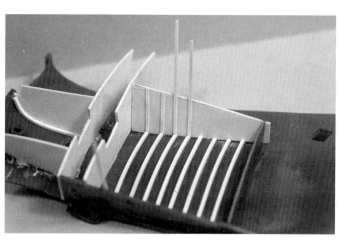

Fig. 1-20. The remaining interior sides have been installed and the interior ribbing is being attached. Use long strips, which are easy to handle, and glue into place. When the glue is dry, simply cut to the correct length.

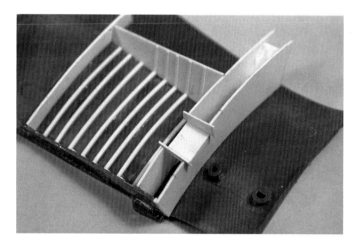

Fig. 1-21. Here the final parts are being added to the interior area.

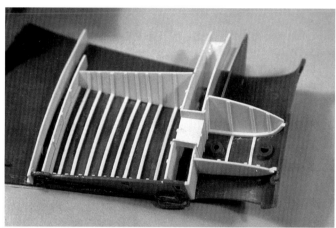

Fig. 1-22. Here the completed interior along with all its ribbing detail is finally ready.

Fig. 1-23. Both sides of the interior landing gear wheel wells of this F4U Corsair are now complete. The secret to duplicating left and right sides is to work with both halves at the same time, completing each step of the construction process before proceeding to the next one. While the parts don't need to be exactly the same, by working in tandem you will get very close.

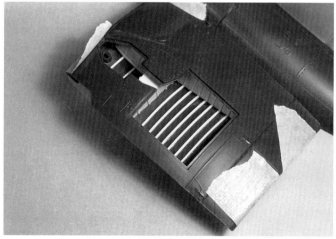

Fig. 1-24. As a final check, the completed landing gear wheel well is positioned in place to show how all the interior detail will appear.

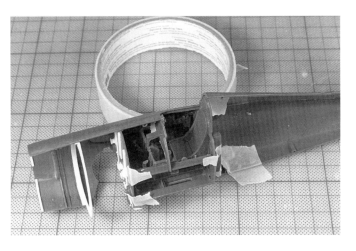

Fig. 1-25. If you plan to do a complete scratchbuild job on a cockpit, I recommend that you tape all the kit's cockpit parts in place so that you get a visual appreciation of the cockpit. This is also the time to start taking measurements of parts so that you know how much space you will have to work with.

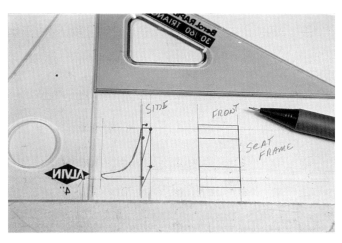

Fig. 1-26. If the aircraft has a seat frame, this is usually a good place to start when beginning a scratchbuilt interior. The first step in making a seat frame is to draw the side and front views.

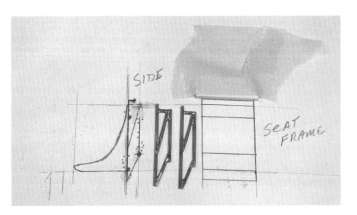

Fig. 1-27. Next set the individual parts in place on top of the drawing, using pins to hold the parts in place. As you set the part apply a tiny amount of super glue to each joint, using a thin wire as an applicator. Gluing the joints as you build up the seat frame helps the pins hold everything in place.

Fig. 1-28. Once the sides are completed, position them on the front view drawing. Again position the parts with pins and then glue the cross-sectional members in place.

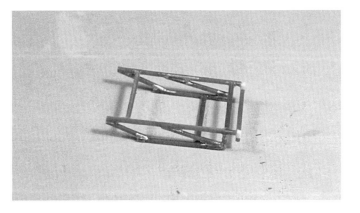

Fig. 1-29. The completed seat frame is now ready for taking measurements for the seat. Also note that Testor's silver paint was applied to the joints to ensure that the super glue was applied all the way around each connection point.

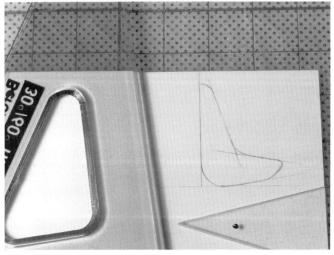

Fig. 1-30. The first step in scratchbuilding a seat is to draw one side of the seat.

Fig. 1-31. Once you are satisfied with the shape of the seat side, carefully cut it out and shape it with a Flex-I-File sanding stick.

Fig. 1-32. Now use this side piece as a pattern for the other side. Trace the pattern and then cut out the part.

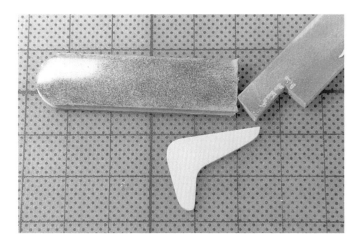

Fig. 1-33. Glue both halves together with white (Elmer's) glue, and then shape them so that they are exactly the same.

Fig. 1-34. Draw the seat backing onto sheet stock. The length of the drawing should include seat back and bottom. The sheet stock should be no more than .010 inch in thickness.

Fig. 1-35. Position strips of balsa wood along the sides of the drawing and tape them into place. You also need to secure the sheet stock that has the drawing on it. Next carefully position the sides of the seat and run a bead of super glue applied with a thin wire applicator along the edge of the joint.

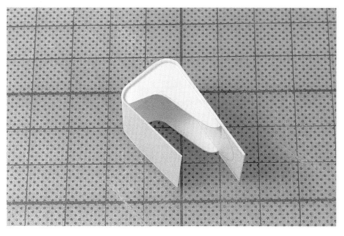

Fig. 1-36. Rough-cut the seat and then roll the plastic sheeting around the seat base, gluing it as you roll. This is why the seat backing needs to be made of thin sheet stock.

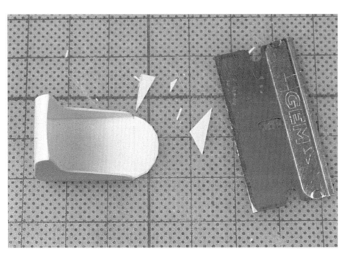

Fig. 1-37. Run beads of super glue along all the interior and exterior joints and then trim off the excess plastic.

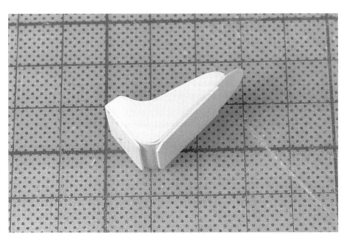

Fig. 1-39. To reinforce the thin plastic sheeting and to represent bulletproof steel plating, glue thicker sections of sheet stock in place on the back and bottom of the seat.

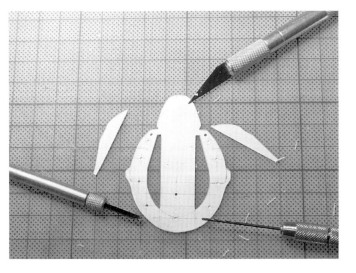

Fig. 1-41. Next the interior openings of the rear bulkhead were drawn and then cut out.

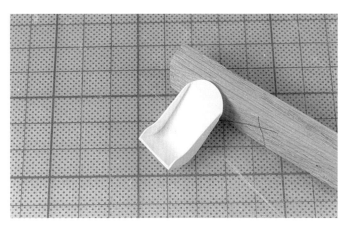

Fig. 1-38. Carefully sand the sides to smooth out the plastic joints by running the sides along stationary pieces of 400- to 600-grit sandpaper.

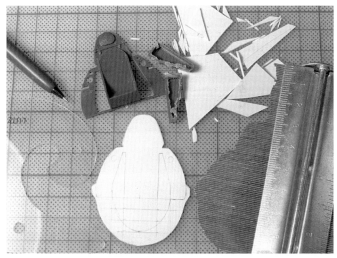

Fig. 1-40. Scratchbuilding the rear cockpit bulkhead is the first big step in building up the rest of the interior. Here a contour gauge, the kit's bulkhead, and a French curve were all used to shape the part. The outer edges of the shape were also form-fit into the fuselage so that it would fit very tightly in place.

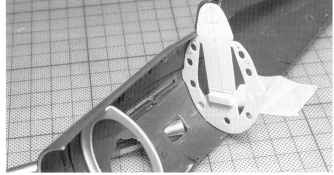

Fig. 1-42. Here the round openings in the bulkhead have been added. To ensure that they are symmetric on both sides, carefully measure and draw the locations of the center points of these openings.

15

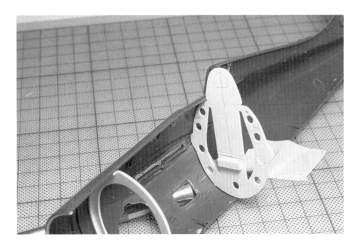

Fig. 1-43. The new rear bulkhead is given a final fit check before proceeding to the next step.

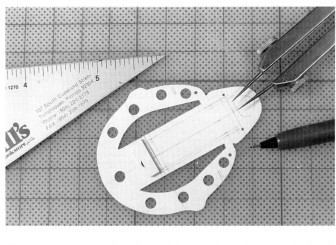

Fig. 1-44. Drawing the locations of the seat frame bars and the head cushion ensures that all these parts will fit into place correctly.

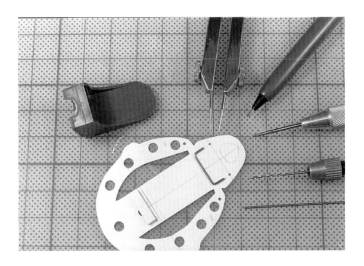

Fig. 1-45. Holes are drilled to accept the seat frame bars, and the brass wire is cut to length and bent into the correct shape.

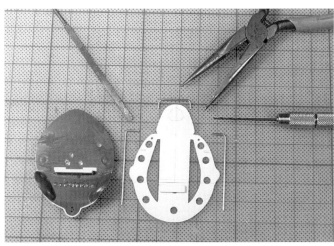

Fig. 1-46. The seat frame bars are all bent to shape and are ready to be installed at the appropriate time in the assembly sequence.

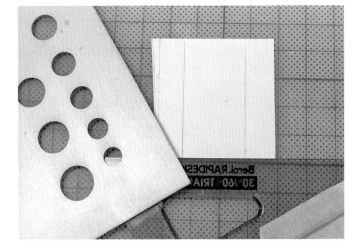

Fig. 1-47. Once the rear bulkhead is complete the next step is to make the floor. Securing a piece of sheet stock to your cutting board and then setting up small triangles to help you draw straight lines at the correct angles will always guarantee you a good part.

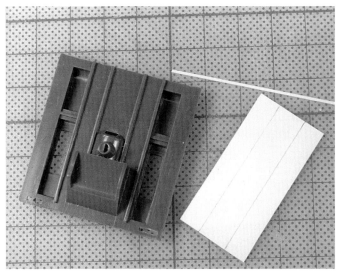

Fig. 1-48. Using the kit's flooring to help design a new one helps make the job easier.

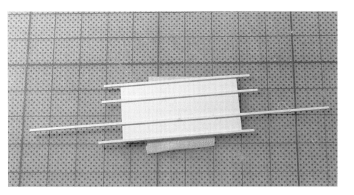

Fig. 1-49. The floor's raised framing is easily added using extra long strips of strip stock. This allows you to easily position the strips in place along predrawn lines.

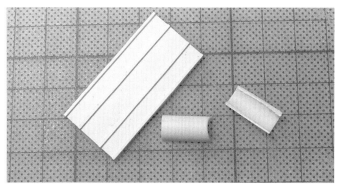

Fig. 1-50. Many control stick bases had cone-shaped covers to protect the mechanisms that connected to them. To reproduce this simply cut tube stock in half.

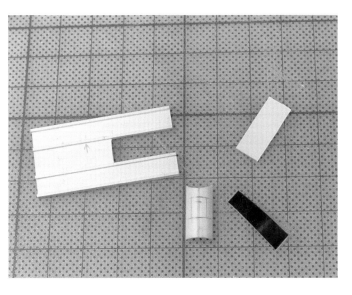

Fig. 1-51. To reproduce the opening that the control stick sits in draw the outline of the hole that you need using a small length of labeling tape.

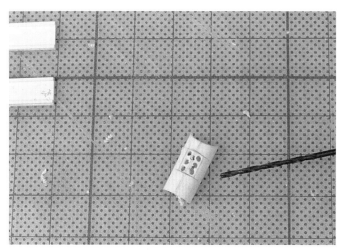

Fig. 1-52. Next drill small pilot holes inside the area to be removed and then cut and shape the remaining plastic using the tip of a no. 11 X-acto blade.

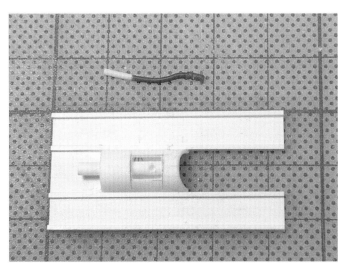

Fig. 1-53. Adding rod stock to lengthen the kit's control stick saved time instead of scratchbuilding a new one.

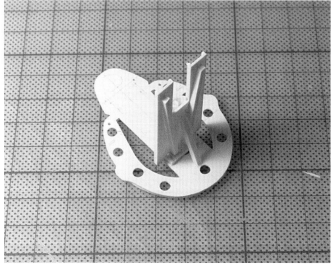

Fig. 1-54. The flooring is glued to the rear bulkhead and reinforcing strips are added to the underside of the floor where they cannot be seen.

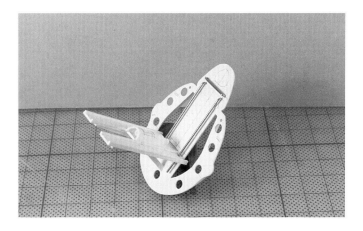

Fig. 1-55. The seat tube framing is getting one last fit check. At this point the cockpit interior is starting to take shape.

Fig. 1-56. Here the newly scratchbuilt part is positioned inside the fuselage along with the modified forward kit-supplied bulkhead. The two parts were glued together and then removed from the fuselage so that the remaining cockpit parts could be scratchbuilt and added.

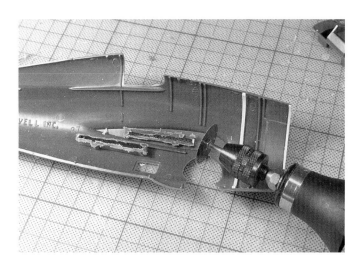

Fig. 1-57. Scratchbuilding cockpits typically calls for some major surgery to the interior areas so that all the scratchbuilt parts will fit into place. Here a motor tool with a circular saw attached has removed a large interior section that would have been very time-consuming to do by hand.

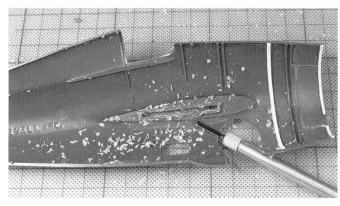

Fig. 1-58. The remaining plastic is scraped flat using a small stencil X-acto blade.

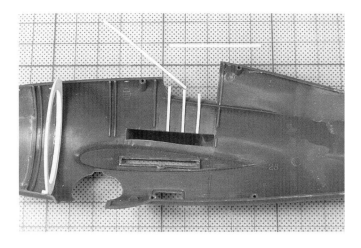

Fig. 1-59. Interior ribbing also needs to be added and here again using small thin strips that are oversize in length helps locate them correctly.

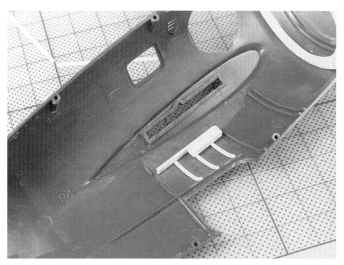

Fig. 1-60. Once the framing is cut to shape, additional lengths of strip stock are added to start forming the interior shapes.

Fig. 1-61. Before we go on to scratchbuilding other interior parts, let's review how to set up interior framing. When adding interior ribbing and other shapes you need to draw the free space areas onto the side of the fuselage where strips will go. To do this you need to locate the cockpit parts in place.

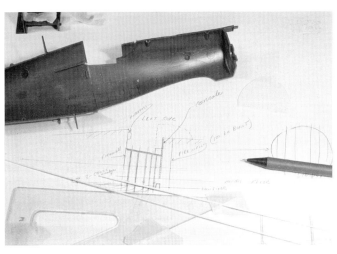

Fig. 1-62. Draw an interior picture of the cockpit and then draw in the locations of the framing.

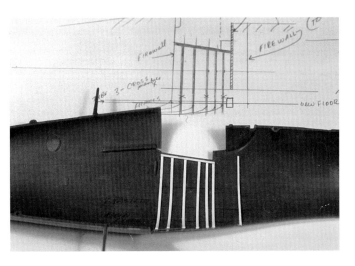

Fig. 1-63. Use the picture that you drew to locate the framing and draw these lines onto the inside area of the fuselage sides, using labeling tape to set the initial lines.

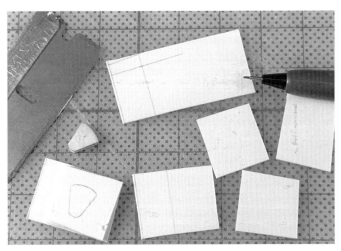

Fig. 1-64. The first step in making a throttle quadrant is to get the correct thickness. Using super glue, fasten layers of sheet plastic together to achieve the thickness that you need.

Fig. 1-65. Rough-cut the shape of the throttle quadrant and then sand it to the correct shape.

Fig. 1-66. The next step is to cut channels into the top of the throttle quadrant to accept the levers. To do this, sandwich the part between two strips of balsa wood, install it in a vise, and then use a razor saw to cut the channels.

Fig. 1-67. Here, two throttle quadrants with channels cut in them are ready for the next step, which is to make the throttle handles and levers.

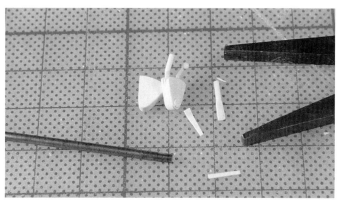

Fig. 1-68. Use combinations of rod and strip plastic to make the levers. Flat-nose pliers are great for flattening out plastic rod, and white glue applied to the tips of the levers will simulate levers that have balls for tips.

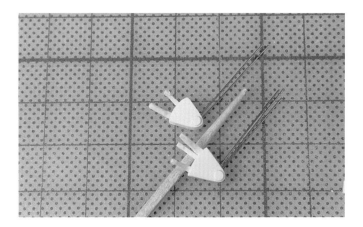

Fig. 1-69. The last step in making throttle quadrants is to add the control cables. Thin lengths of brass wire work great to simulate these stiff cables. Simply drill small holes into the sides of the quadrant and then glue the brass wire into place. Cut the brass wire in long lengths so that you can form-fit them into the fuselage when it's time to glue them into place.

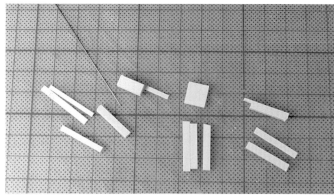

Fig. 1-70. The next step in scratchbuilding is to build up the switch, radio, and electrical boxes as well as adding parts such as switches, dials, and hand cranks. I assemble pieces of various sizes and lengths of plastic strip to begin this process. These bits and pieces of plastic will soon become shapes that will form the left and right side cockpit details.

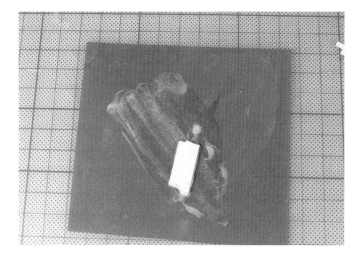

Fig. 1-71. Glue three small lengths of plastic together and smooth the sides by running the piece across sandpaper.

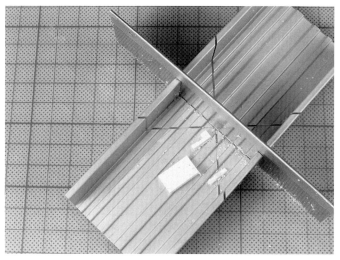

Fig. 1-72. The next step is to cut the newly formed shape to size. To do this use a miter box and a razor saw.

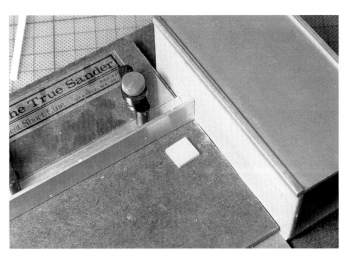

Fig. 1-73. To ensure that the edges are square use a Northline true sander to lightly sand the edges. This handy little device is used by the model railroad community and it works well for scratchbuilding aircraft parts.

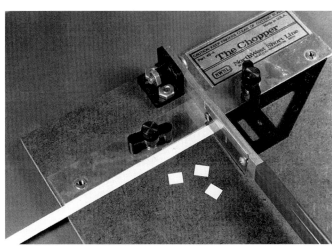

Fig. 1-74. Another great model railroader's tool is the Northline true chopper. This gem will duplicate shapes and angles and is a must for scratchbuilding.

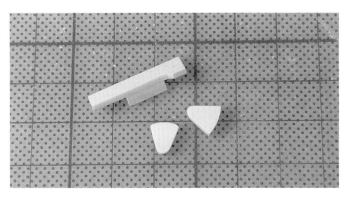

Fig. 1-75. The left side console has been shaped using three different sizes of plastic stock, the larger of which is a small length of Evergreen channel stock. This is also the side where the throttle quadrants will be attached.

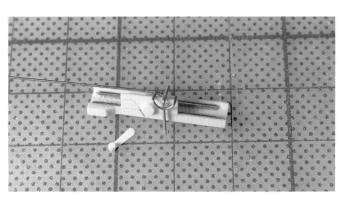

Fig. 1-76. Brass wire has been added to the underside of the left console to strengthen it, and small thin lengths of brass wire have been shaped and attached. A dial, as well as the handle tip on the crank arm, were made using Waldron's punch tool.

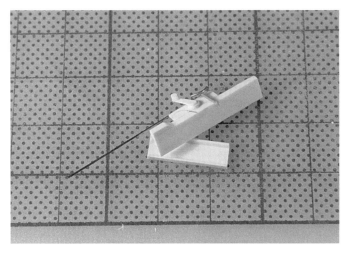

Fig. 1-77. Here the crank arm has been attached and a length of brass wire has been added to represent the cable attachment for the lever arm.

Fig. 1-78. The right side console and radio and switch boxes start out as simple box shapes glued to a length of strip stock.

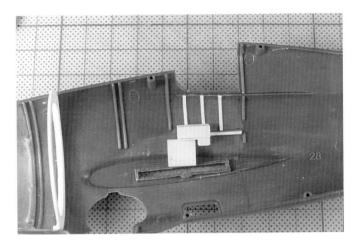

Fig. 1-79. As you are building up these parts always check your work to ensure that it will fit into its location. This is a trial and error process and you may have to modify the part several times to get it just right.

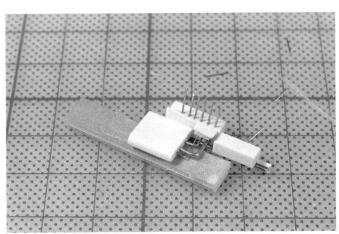

Fig. 1-80. At this point several different diameters of brass wire have been added to represent cabling and plumbing. Lengths of thin brass wire have been glued in place at the location of the switch banks.

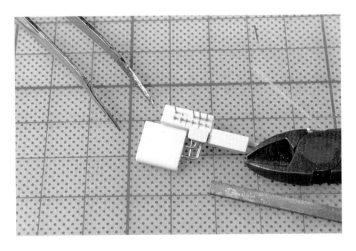

Fig. 1-81. The thin brass lengths are then cut to length using a sharp set of small wire cutters.

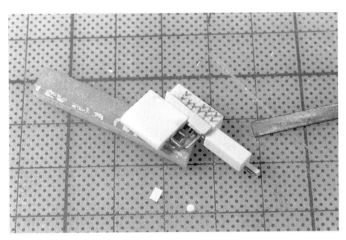

Fig. 1-82. Once all the brass wire lengths are cut to size use a micro file to give the tips of the wire a flat look.

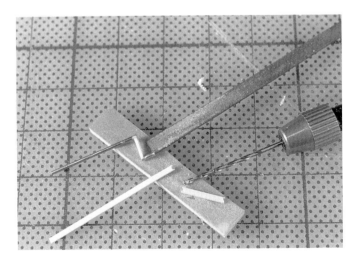

Fig. 1-83. Making a large crank handle is as easy as it appears. The trick is to drill into the ends of the arm so that the brass wire will seat into the plastic, forming a good strong bond.

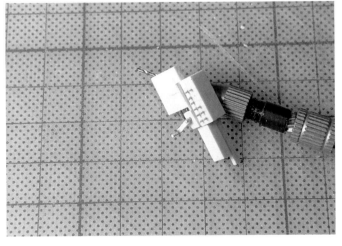

Fig. 1-84. The large crank has been installed on the right side console and the part is now ready for installation between the rear and forward bulkheads.

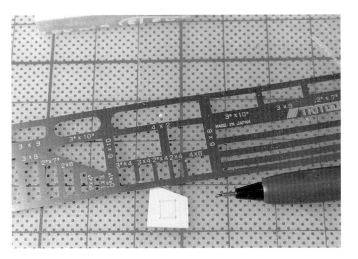

Fig. 1-85. To make small raised surface shapes use your scribing template to draw these outlines and then cut them out.

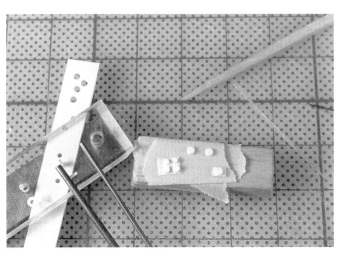

Fig. 1-86. Dials can easily be made using Waldron's punch tool. The edges of these small disks will have small burrs; to get the disks to sit flat, run them across a stationary piece of 600-grit sandpaper with your finger.

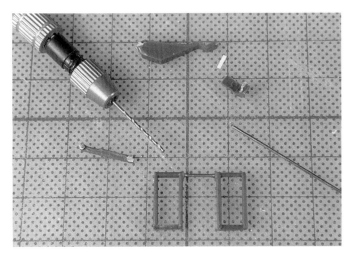

Fig. 1-87. Wherever possible I like to use kit parts in my scratchbuilding efforts. Here the rudder pedal frames from the kit have been modified and a length of brass wire has been glued between them.

Fig. 1-88. Making curved rudder pedal shapes is easy if you have different diameter wood dowels and some sandpaper.

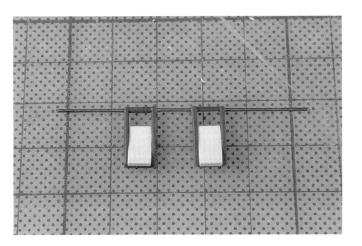

Fig. 1-89. The new rudder pedals have been installed into the pedal frames and wire lengths have also been added to the outer ends. The long length of wire will help set the part in place.

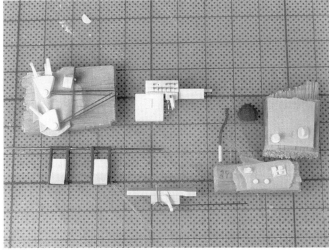

Fig. 1-90. All the subassemblies for this scratchbuilding project are now complete, and all that is left is to assemble them and also to make the console.

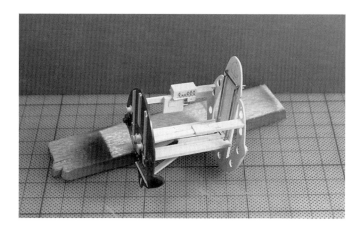

Fig. 1-91. The right side console has been attached between the rear and forward bulkheads and the left side is next. To set the right and left sides correctly, the entire section is set into the left and then the right fuselage halves so that the parts can be positioned correctly.

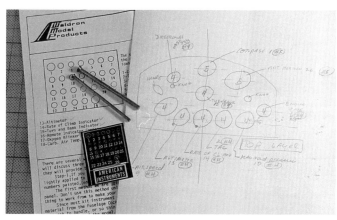

Fig. 1-92. The first step in making the console is to draw a picture of the console and identify all the instruments that you will need. For this console I used Waldron's instrument faces, but Reheat Models dial decals also work great for these types of scratch-building efforts.

Fig. 1-93. The next step is to draw the console shapes onto sheet plastic and then start locating the dial faces on the console.

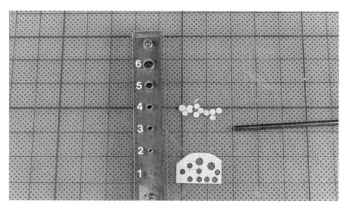

Fig. 1-94. Cut out the console and then punch out the holes where the individual instruments will go. The size punch you use must be coordinated with the size of the instrument. Write this information on the drawing that you made to lessen your chances of a mistake.

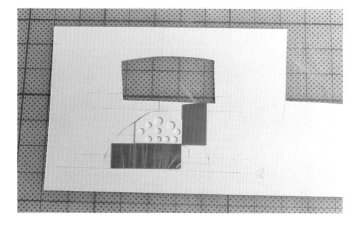

Fig. 1-95. The next step for this console is to glue it to the larger backing so that the entire console will be formed. Labeling tape was set in place on the drawing to ensure that the smaller console faces were correctly positioned onto the larger part.

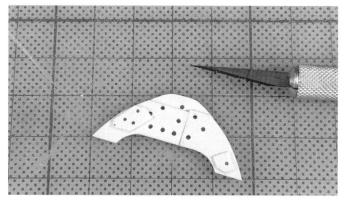

Fig. 1-96. Sometimes consoles are made from more than one or two parts and you may want to add extra material to the back side to help strengthen it. The holes that are drilled through the console will allow the white glue that will be used to attach the instruments to the front of the console to seep out the back.

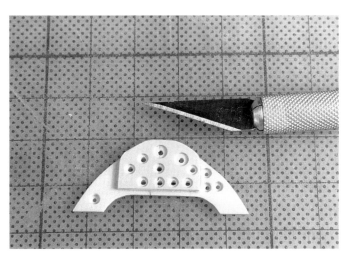

Fig. 1-97. Here the completed console is ready to be painted. After painting, you'll insert the instrument faces into the holes.

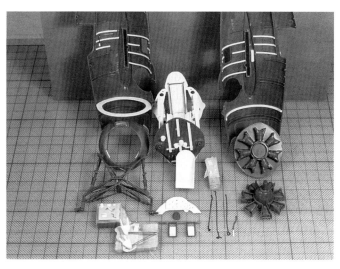

Fig. 1-98. Here are all the parts for this F4F Wildcat, and they are ready for painting and installation.

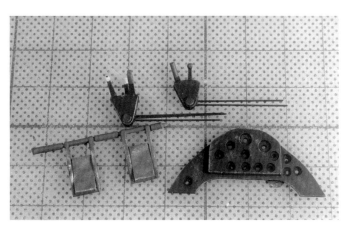

Fig. 1-99. As smaller parts are completed you can paint and weather them.

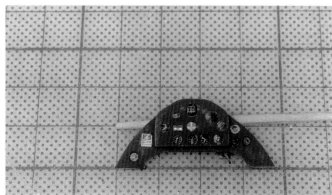

Fig. 1-100. The completed instrument console with a small instruction plate added. Waldron as well as several other companies make these small instrument plates from thin sheet aluminum or with decals.

Fig. 1-101. Another way to make a good-looking console is to take the kit's part and sand it down to get it to a thickness at which the Waldron punch tool can punch holes through it. This saves you the time in making a new console, but it works only if the kit's part is an accurate size.

Fig. 1-102. First draw the instrument locations on the face of the thinned kit console and then punch out the holes.

Fig. 1-103. A backing for the console was made, small holes were drilled for the white glue to seep out, and small framing was added to the switch banks across the top rim of the console.

Fig. 1-104. The modified kit's console looks much more realistic and it only took some patience and a little time.

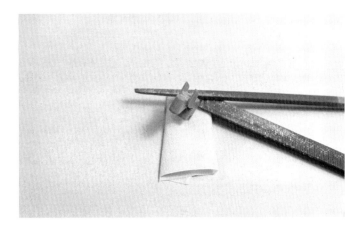

Fig. 1-105. Sometimes kit-supplied gunsights can be modified to make them appear much more realistic. The center section of the plastic of this P40 gunsight was removed with micro files so that the edges will become the frame of the reflecting glass.

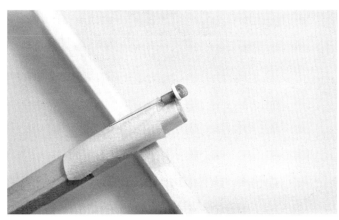

Fig. 1-106. Scratchbuilding gunsights is easy. This gunsight was made from two small lengths of plastic tubing, a small stick of Evergreen strip stock shaped in a semicircle, and a piece of brass wire.

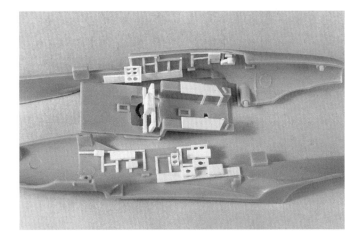

Fig. 1-107. Even 1/72 scale aircraft can have scratchbuilt interiors. About 50 cents worth of Evergreen plastic was all that was needed to enhance the appearance of the interior of Fujimi's Gekko Model 21 Nightfighter. Model by Scott Weller.

Fig. 1-108. Even 1/72 scale scratchbuilt projects need fit checks to ensure that all the parts fit in place correctly. While this is a small kit, the scratchbuilt parts are clearly evident. Model by Scott Weller.

Fig. 1-109. The first step in applying seatbelts is to paint and weather the seat.

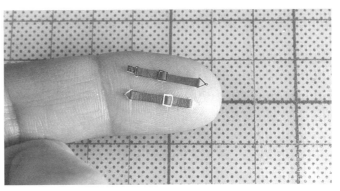

Fig. 1-110. Seatbelts were made from masking tape and painted with Polly S earthbrown color. The seatbelt hardware is from Model Technologies. While photoetched seatbelts that come complete as one piece are easy to install, using separate hardware for the seatbelts and seat buckles on 1/32 or 1/48 scale aircraft definitely gives the seatbelts a three-dimensional appearance.

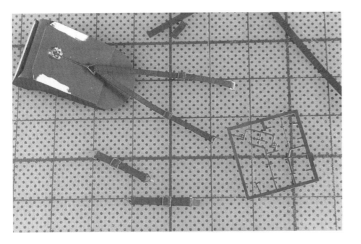

Fig. 1-111. The shoulder harnesses are easily made with a long piece of masking tape cut and painted. The length of the seatbelt needs to be bent in half and positioned through the rear hardware frame before the adjusting buckles and clips are attached.

Fig. 1-112. To get the seatbelts to lie correctly fold them over the rims of the seats and then glue them in place with tiny amounts of super glue.

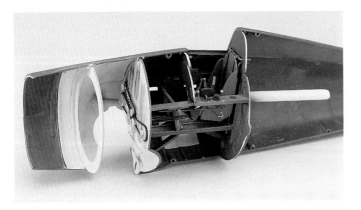

Fig. 1-113. The seat has been positioned into the scratchbuilt cockpit and the shoulder harnesses has been brought over the top of the rear seat frame. The completed cockpit has been painted and weathered and is ready to be installed in the fuselage. Photo by Glenn Johnson.

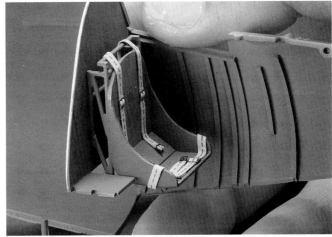

Fig. 1-114. Seatbelts don't always have to be brown. The seatbelts on this F4U Corsair were painted white and the center lines on the seatbelts were done with a 000 inking pen. Photo by Glenn Johnson.

WORKING WITH RESIN, WHITE-METAL, AND PHOTOETCHED DETAIL SETS

Over the past few years there has been an incredible explosion in the variety of resin and white-metal detail and conversion sets that are available to the modeler. Before we go into our discussion of working with resin, white metal, and photoetch, let's talk about how these conversion and detail sets are made. Resin and white-metal detail sets are manufactured very differently from injection-molded kits in a process that is very labor-intensive. The first step is to scratchbuild a set of masters from materials such as basswood, plastic, and brass. The designer of the master patterns needs to engineer how the parts will fit together, how they will be cast, whether resin or white metal will be used, and how they will fit on the modeling subject. Once the master patterns are complete, a set of molds is made from liquid RTV rubber. The molds are specifically engineered for the master pattern parts and this can be a very intensive trial and error process. Once the molds are complete, a set of castings are made and the castings are checked to see if any changes are needed to the master patterns or the castings. If adjustments to either the master patterns or the molds are necessary new molds will need to be created. Once the designer is satisfied with the master patterns and the resulting casting, instructions are developed and the kits are then produced, packaged, and marketed. There is no automation in the mold making or casting process; it is all done manually, which adds a great deal of expense to the overall price of the detail set. In addition, mold making and casting are usually done using a pressure or vacuum chamber, which adds to the time, effort, and expense required to produce a kit. Now you know what it takes to make conversion or detail sets and why they cost almost as much as the kits do.

Photoetched detail sets are not as complicated to produce or as labor-intensive, which is why they are fairly inexpensive. The toughest part of photoetch designing is to ensure that any parts that need to be bent into shape fit together correctly and that all the individual parts and subassemblies fit into their respective locations correctly. Part fitting is especially important with interior detail sets. The designer uses either a computer drawing program or manually draws the parts. Once the design is complete and ready for initial manufacturing, it is imprinted onto a brass or stainless steel plate and this metal is then given a chemical bath. The chemical bath removes the metal from all areas except where the imprint is, and what is left is the photoetched detail set. The parts are then tested for a final fit check, adjustments are made, and then the photoetched sheet goes into full production.

Working with resin is easy as long as you follow a few simple guidelines. First and foremost, you need to be very careful when removing resin pour plugs from parts. Resin is easy to cut and sand, so be careful not to overdo it. I recommend cutting the resin plugs down to as small an area as possible using a razor saw and then sanding the remaining resin off. The excess resin on parts can be easily sanded off by running the part across a stationary piece of sandpaper. Be sure to rotate the part so that you do not sand off too much resin on one side. Be sure that you wear a dust mask when sanding resin, as the resin dust particles should not be inhaled. One way to avoid the resin dust problem is to use waterproof sandpaper and wet-sand the parts. Once you get the excess resin off, wash the parts with mild soap and warm water to remove any mold release agents.

Resin parts sometimes have tiny voids or air bubbles, which will need to be filled. While the quality of resin castings for aircraft models is very good, you still get an occasional void or air bubble. While some modelers may complain about these occasional problems, I look at it this way: Injection-molded models have seams to repair, mold seam lines to scrape off, and indentations to fill; and resin parts have pour plugs and occasional voids and air bubbles. It's six of one and half a dozen of the other. Personally I like parts such as resin tires, especially ones with treads, because you do not have to repair the tread detail after you deal with the seam, which is exactly what you would be doing if the tire were from an injection-molded kit.

Voids or air bubbles can easily be filled with super glue or putty or even Evergreen strip stock. For voids on flat or large curved surfaces use Duro's blue tube super glue. This thick gel glue works great as a filler. Testor's plastic modelers putty also works well for these voids. For small air bubbles use very thin super glue applied with a thin wire applicator. Sometimes the air bubbles will be so small that the surface tension of the super glue will not allow the glue to seep into the tiny area. In these cases, slightly enlarge the hole with a drill bit. Super glue accelerator will not affect resin, so you can use it to speed up the drying process of the super glue. You can also use Evergreen strip stock on small shapes, in corners, on edges, or on the rims of circular shapes. Use a strip size which fits into the hole, dip the tip of the plastic in a puddle of super glue, and insert the tip of the strip into the hole. When the glue is dry, cut the plastic and trim and sand to shape. Sometime parts may also be warped or bent and these can be corrected by submerging the part in hot tap water and then straightening the part out. You will need to secure the part in its new position until it cools down; otherwise it may snap back to its former shape, as resin sometimes has a shape memory. You can also use a hair dryer, but be careful not to melt or distort the part. If you do not feel comfortable trying to fix the problem, return the kit, as most resin manufacturers will gladly replace the kit or the defective part.

Once you have fixed any problems, clean the parts again to remove dirt and resin dust, give them a final cleaning with Polly S paint preparation cleaner, and then give them a coat of primer. The primer will act as a final check for any voids or bubbles that you may have missed. They are easy to miss, especially with light-colored resin parts; your eyes have a tendency to become "snow blind" when looking at the parts because of their light color. Once the parts are completed you are ready for their final painting and assembly.

Resin will sometimes shrink, and while some master pattern makers account for this when making their master parts, some do not. Shrinkage can be somewhat of a problem on resin control surfaces, but the solution is easy. Usually the width of the control surface is slightly shorter and all you need to do is add a layer of Evergreen sheet stock to the ends of the control surfaces and then form-fit them into place.

White-metal parts are also very easy to work with, as they can be scraped, sanded, and shaped just like plastic. White metal, like resin, can have mold release agents on it, so give it a good cleaning with an enamel-base paint thinner. Sometimes the surfaces of white metal can have minute voids, which can easily be filled with super glue. White-metal parts typically have very small seam lines much as injection-molded parts do, although they can be difficult to see because of the shiny appearance of the metal. Scrape and sand the white-metal seam lines just as if they were plastic. When you are satisfied with your work give the parts a shot of primer. The gray color will highlight any seam lines that you may have missed. To get the primer to blend in, sand the surface with 600-grit sandpaper, coat the bare area with primer, and then give the entire part a complete coat of primer. White-metal parts are very flexible and as a consequence are sometimes bent when you get them. Have no fear, though, as they are easily bent back into shape. A word of caution here—white-metal landing gear may not be as strong as injection-molded gears are, and over time the gear may begin to sag. This does not happen on all types of white-metal landing gear parts and it depends on the thickness of the metal, the weight of the model, and the type of metal mixture the white metal is composed of.

The first step in using photoetch is to clean the surfaces by running the photoetched sheet across a stationary sheet of sandpaper. A light touch is all that is needed to clean up the metal, and when it is shiny it's clean. Always cut photoetch with a sharp blade and cut the parts on a hard surface such as a glass plate. Generally, it is easier to cut a photoetched part off its tree by leaving a little of the stub attached to the part. You can easily remove the remaining stub from the part with a Flex-I-File sanding stick. Stainless steel photoetched parts can be more difficult to cut off their trees because the metal is very strong, but this strength can be an advantage. Brass, on the other hand, is very bendable and soft, which can also be advantageous. To get curves in photoetch, simply bend the part around a wood dowel or other round object that has a diameter slightly smaller than the diameter that you need. You need to use a slightly smaller diameter when you are bending the photoetch into shape because the photoetch will spring back a little.

Sharp bends and angles can be achieved using a set of flat needle-nose pliers or by using two single-edge razor blades. When gluing photoetch be sure that the gluing surface is shiny. For cleaning edges, run a Flex-I-File sanding stick back and forth across the edge a couple of times to clean it. Super glue is an excellent bonding agent for both brass and stainless steel photoetch and when strength is not an issue, white glue also works great. Using white glue will allow you some flexibility in positioning the pieces together correctly. White glue is also an excellent filler for cracks and voids when using photoetch. Photoetch should also be primed prior to any finish painting. To strengthen photoetched shapes such as boxes and corners, use small lengths of Evergreen strip and round stock cut to size and glued to the inside areas of these delicate parts. Another benefit is that the strip stock can act as a handling stem so that you can more easily position the part.

Conversion parts that require major surgery to the aircraft such as cutting off the wing tip to add wing tanks, adding a new nose piece, or cutting out the center section of a fuselage or wing and adding a new piece are easy if you have a few simple tools, plan your work, remember to think about what you are doing, and go slow. Just about all the resin conversion sets are painstakingly engineered and they usually fit very well. It is always a good idea to reinforce these types of parts so that they are firmly secured to the plastic. If you are adding a new nose piece or cutting out a center section of a fuselage or wing and adding a new piece, it's a good idea to add a strip of Evergreen strip stock around the perimeter of the inside of the kit so that there will be a larger gluing surface. Parts that are heavy and hanging such as wing tip tanks can be reinforced by filling the tip of the wing area with resin or super glue and then setting lengths of brass wire into the connection points between the wing tip tank and the wing area. These are simple tricks that will ensure that the heavy parts you add do not break off, which would really ruin your day, especially after you invested so much time in finishing the model.

\Fig. 2-1. The first step in working with resin tires is to remove the part from the pour blocks. The easy way to do this is to use a razor saw and cut as close to the part as possible.

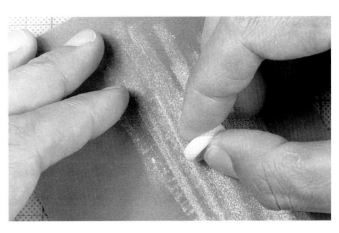

Fig. 2-2. Next, hold the tire flat and run it across a stationary piece of sandpaper to remove the remaining resin.

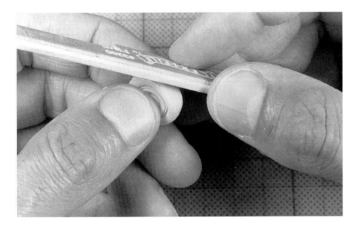

Fig. 2-3. Clean the edges around the flattened portion of the tire with a Flex-I-File sanding stick.

Fig. 2-4. To get the correct diameter of the landing gear wheel stem, use calipers or a similar device to measure the diameter and then drill the appropriate size holes in the resin wheels. If you drill a bad hole, simply fill it with super glue, let it dry, and then re-drill.

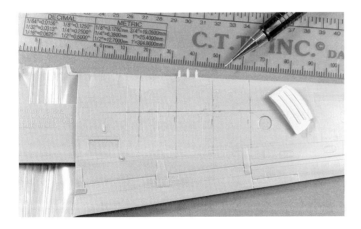

Fig. 2-5. To add detail resin sets to the wings, you need to set a grid on the wing to properly locate all the parts.

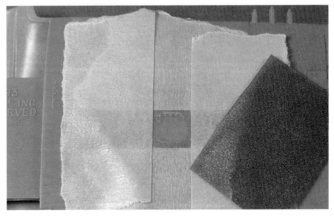

Fig. 2-6. Sand off any surface detail that would interfere with the attachment of the wing parts. Use masking tape to protect any surrounding detail.

Fig. 2-7. To contour the parts correctly to the wing, place a piece of sandpaper on the surface of the wing, hold it stationary, then run the part back and forth across the wing at the approximate location where it would be attached.

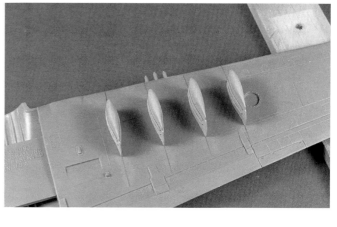

Fig. 2-8. Once all the wing details are added, check the bases where they attach to the wing, and fill in any voids you find with white glue.

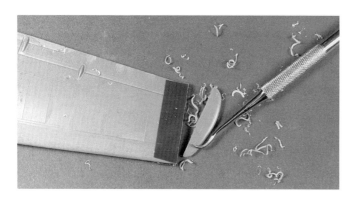

Fig. 2-9. The first step in installing wing tip tanks is to cut off the end of the wing. Use a piece of labeling tape to guide your scriber or razor saw.

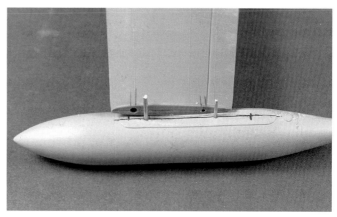

Fig. 2-10. Since resin wing tip tanks are usually fairly heavy, I recommend that you reinforce their attachment points to the wing with brass wire. First drill the holes in the wing tip tanks, set the brass rod in place, then mark and drill the holes in the tip of the wing.

Fig. 2-11. To fill in the seam area between the wing tip tank and the edge of the wing, fill the void with white glue and contour it with a damp Q-tip.

Fig. 2-12. After the white glue dries there will be small air pockets. Simply fill these with additional applications of white glue.

Fig. 2-13. Once you are sure that the voids and air pockets are filled, check the attachment point with Testor's silver paint.

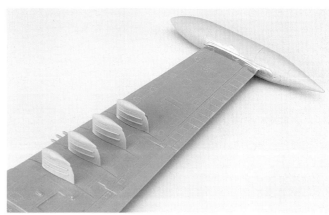

Fig. 2-14. The completely modified wing with the undercarriage details and wing tip tank are now ready to be attached to the fuselage. Photo by Glenn Johnson.

Fig. 2-15. To clean up large resin detail parts and flatten their attachment surfaces, run them across a stationary piece of sand-paper. Use a figure-eight motion or rotate the part to insure that you do not remove too much resin on one side or edge.

Fig. 2-16. To cut out fuselage sections, set labeling tape along the edges of cut lines and use Bare Metal Foil's plastic scriber to cut through the plastic.

Fig. 2-17. Glue the resin part in place and fill the edges with super glue. After it's dry, sand the area and contour the shape of the fuselage.

Fig. 2-18. Additional coats of super glue will most likely be necessary in order to fix the tiny cracks and voids around the inserted part. Be careful when sanding resin, as it is much softer than plastic and consequently it sands very easily.

Fig. 2-19. A final check with Testor's silver paint should always be done after major surgery on either fuselages or wings.

Fig. 2-21. The fuselage and new nosepiece have been contoured and additional super glue has been added around the seam line to fix any remaining problems. Note that the raised panel lines on the surface of the kit's fuselage have been sanded off.

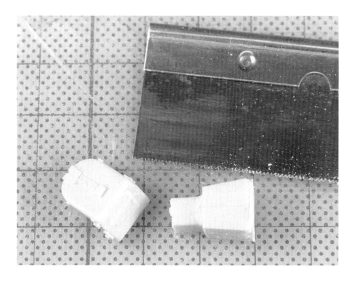

Fig. 2-23. Large resin cockpit detail accessories such as seats usually have large pour plugs, which are easily removed with a razor saw.

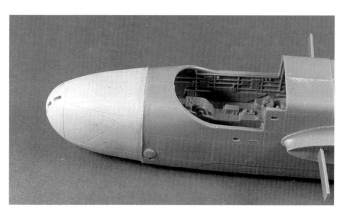

Fig. 2-20. The new nosepiece on this Monogram A26 has been glued into place. The shape of the nosepiece and the fuselage at the attachment point are slightly different along the left and right sides, and will need some heavy sanding work to contour them correctly.

Fig. 2-22. As a final check, here again Testor's silver paint has been applied to the seams to be sure there are no remaining cracks or voids.

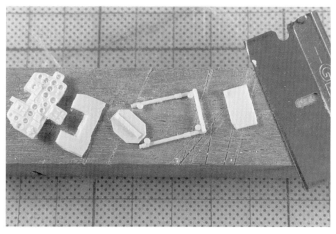

Fig. 2-24. Remove the pour plugs and reinforcing bands from smaller resin parts, using a sharp, single-edge razor blade on a hardwood block.

Fig. 2-25. Once the resin cockpit parts have been cleaned up, tape them together, insert them into the fuselage, and tape up the fuselage to check the fit. This is the time to note any adjustments or changes that need to be made to the resin parts to get them to fit correctly.

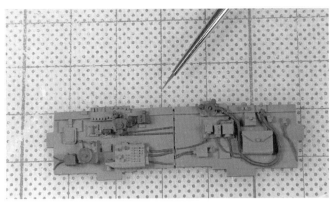

Fig. 2-26. Meteor Productions resin detail set for Academy's 1/48 scale P47N has beautiful interior detail. The first step in highlighting these parts is to paint the base interior color and then start picking out the raised surface details with a small detail brush. Even the wiring on this detail set can be painted because it has a high enough relief to allow the paintbrush to paint the wire's surface.

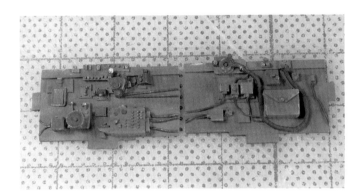

Fig. 2-27. Additional details such as the throttle handles and switches have been painted lighter colors. The edges of the box shapes have been drybrushed with dulled Testor's silver paint, and then the surfaces have been given a light dusting of pastel black for a weathered effect.

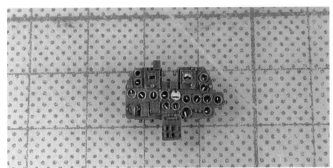

Fig. 2-28. The console on Meteor Productions P47N is beautifully done. It is easy to paint the individual dials with a detail brush because of the raised relief of the individual instruments. A light drybrushing with Testor's silver can really highlight these types of parts.

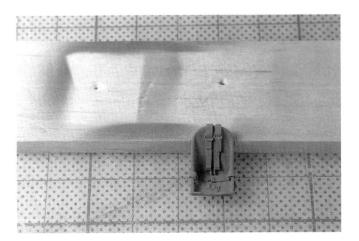

Fig. 2-29. The first step in painting a resin seat is to spray the entire part with the color of the seat.

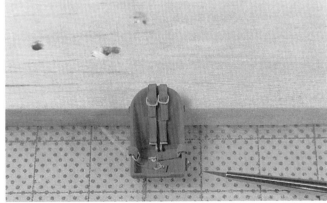

Fig. 2-30. The second step is to paint the seatbelts the correct color. Here again, the seatbelts are raised high enough from the seat to allow easy painting. Next you need to paint the buckles on the adjusting rings on the seatbelts.

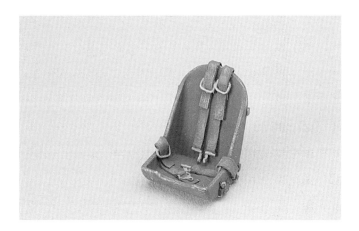

Fig. 2-31. The last step is to weather the seatbelts with a lighter shade of brown, and add dulled silver paint to the edges of the seat to simulate paint wear. Photo by Glenn Johnson.

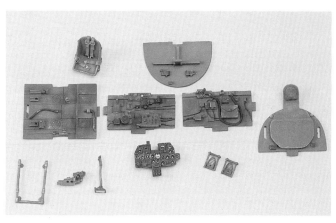

Fig. 2-32. All the resin parts from Meteor Productions for the beautiful P47N detail set have been cleaned, painted, and detailed and are ready to be installed. Photo by Glenn Johnson.

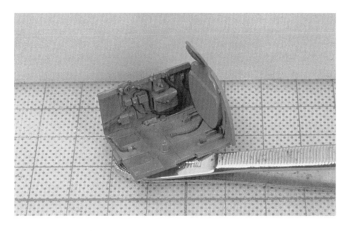

Fig. 2-33. To begin assembling the resin cockpit, work in stages. First set the back and either the right or left side.

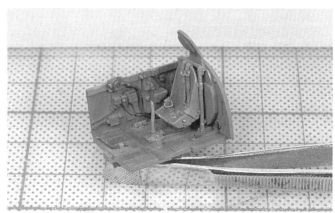

Fig. 2-34. Then add additional interior details such as the seat frame, seat, and control stick.

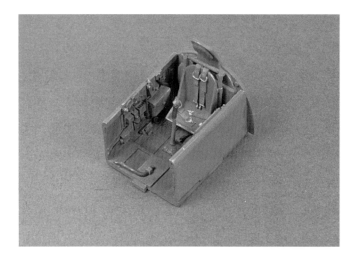

Fig. 2-35. The next step in building up a resin cockpit is to add the other side. To ensure good glue joints be sure to scrape the paint off the gluing surfaces.

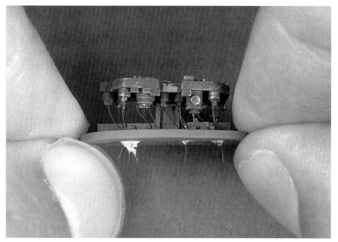

Fig. 2-36. Since the back side of a P47N console is exposed, wiring needs to be added to the back of the console. In 1/48 scale this was done using clear nylon sewing thread that was painted after it was installed.

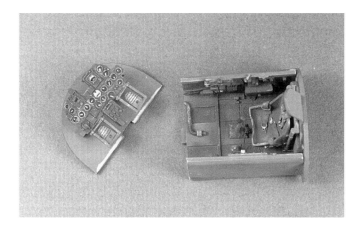

Fig. 2-37. The last step in assembling the cockpit is to put the forward cockpit console wall into place.

Fig. 2-38. Install the resin cockpit into the side of the fuselage in the same way as if it were a kit-supplied part.

Fig. 2-39. The last step in the assembly of this P47N interior is to add the gunsight, which you do after painting the model, adding decals, and applying weathering. The new cockpit interior greatly enhances the appearance of this model.

Fig. 2-40. The first step in attaching new white-metal propellers to a plastic propeller hub is to cut the plastic props carefully from the hub using a sharp knife. Be careful to ensure that you have a flat cut.

Fig. 2-41. To remove white-metal parts from their trees simply cut them off using a single-edge razor blade on a hard surface. The metal is very soft and easily bent, so be careful.

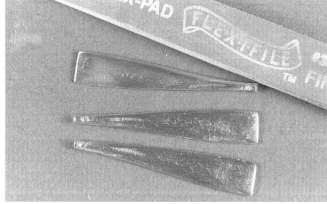

Fig. 2-42. To clean up the surfaces of white metal, sand them with a Flex-I-File sanding stick. To fill in cracks or holes in the white metal simply apply some super glue as a filler and sand smooth.

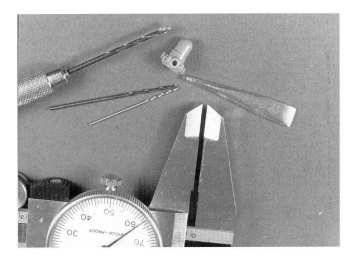

Fig. 2-43. To determine the diameter of the base of the white-metal propeller, use calipers to measure the diameter and then drill the appropriate size opening into the propeller hub. To help set the tip of the drill bit correctly, punch the center of the drill area.

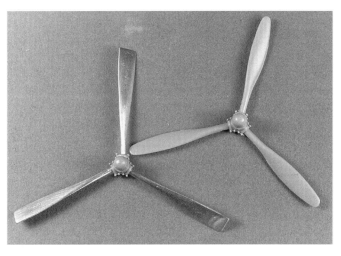

Fig. 2-44. The individual propeller blades were attached with super glue. When gluing them in place, be sure that they are all angled the same with respect to the hub. The new propeller looks very different from the kit-supplied one.

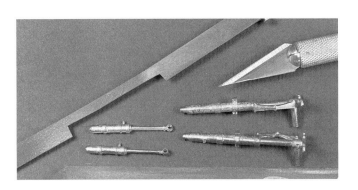

Fig. 2-45. White-metal detail parts such as landing gear sometimes have seams just like plastic ones do, and you can deal with them the same way as plastic parts. Carefully scrape the seams off and then sand the surfaces smooth using a Flex-I-File.

Fig. 2-46. These beautiful white-metal 50-caliber machine guns are made by Koster Aero Enterprises, but like most white-metal parts they are usually bent. Have no fear, as they always straighten out. Here the gun barrel was straightened out by rolling the barrel end along a raised, hard, flat surface and then finishing the job using flat-nose pliers.

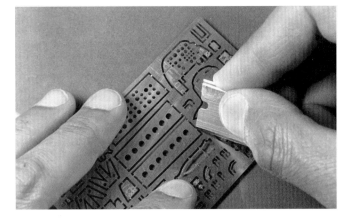

Fig. 2-47. Brass or stainless steel photoetch should always be cut on a hard surface like a glass plate using a sharp knife or razor blade. Be prepared to go through a lot of knife blades when using photoetch.

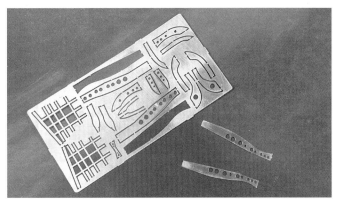

Fig. 2-48. Photoetch also needs to be cleaned. The easiest way to do this is to run the parts across a stationary piece of fine-grit sandpaper.

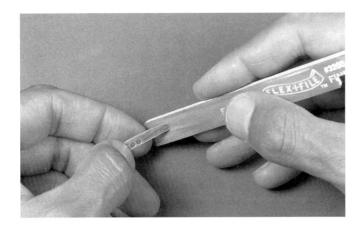

Fig. 2-49. The stub edges also need to be removed on photoetched parts, and the best way to do this is to run the edges across a Flex-I-File sanding stick. If the edges of the photoetch are the gluing surfaces be sure to also run sandpaper across them.

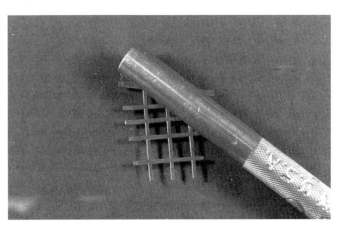

Fig. 2-50. Photoetched parts can be flattened out by running a round dowel across them on a hard surface. You may have to flip the part over several times to get it really flat.

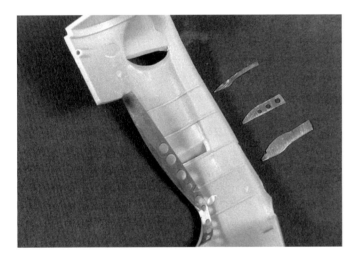

Fig. 2-51. Eduard's 1/48 scale photoetched detail parts on the wheel well of AMT's A-20G Havoc are just about ready to be installed. Super glue works best to attach photoetch to photoetch or photoetch to plastic.

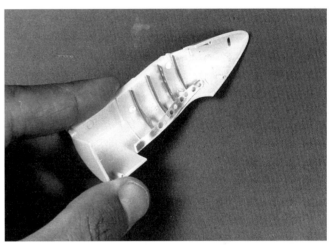

Fig. 2-52. The photoetched framing parts have been attached and the part is now ready to be painted. Be sure when gluing these types of detail parts that they are all straight.

Fig. 2-53. The brass detail parts have been added to the left and right halves, the interior has been painted, and it is ready to be closed up. While photoetched detail sets can add a lot of realism to an aircraft model you need to be careful when installing them. Check the fit of all surrounding parts to ensure that the photoetch does not interfere with them. The lip framing on these detail parts had to be cut on one side and notched on the other to allow for the landing gear frame to sit correctly.

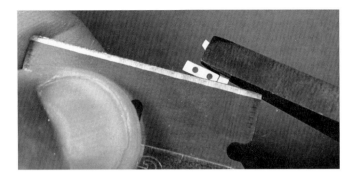

Fig. 2-54. Photoetched cockpit detail sets, especially the Eduard's series, have a lot of small parts that need to be bent into box shapes. The easiest way to ensure good bend lines is to position the part in a set of flat-nose pliers along the bend line and then bend the part using a single-edge razor blade.

Fig. 2-55. These box shape parts were all bent into shape using a combination of single-edge razor blades, flat-nose pliers, and a set of tweezers. The tweezers were used to make fine adjustments.

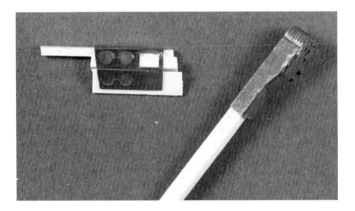

Fig. 2-56. Photoetched box shapes can be very fragile. To make them stronger add lengths of Evergreen strip stock to the inside areas. The plastic will also act as a good gluing surface for the individual parts.

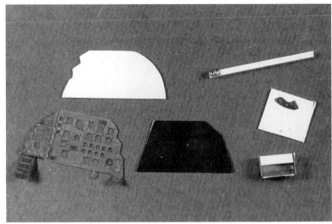

Fig. 2-57. To get the instrument dials on a clear acetate sheet to stand out, cut a backing for the console using white plastic and then sandwich the acetate between the photoetched console and the white plastic backing.

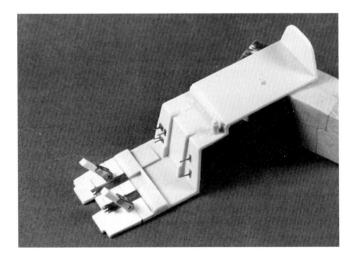

Fig. 2-58. Building up a cockpit using photoetched detail sets is done pretty much the same way as any other detailing project. Work in stages and always check your work. The initial interior parts have been installed on the cockpit flooring of this A-20G Havoc.

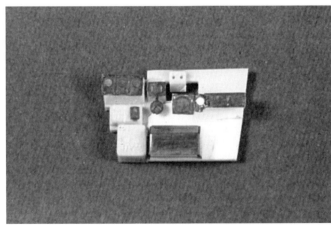

Fig. 2-59. The photoetched parts have been glued to the right side of the cockpit. This part also had to be modified to accept these small photoetched parts.

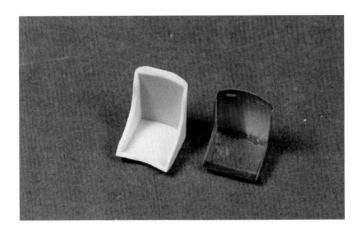

Fig. 2-60. Photoetched seats are also a marked improvement over the thicker, out-of-scale kit-supplied seats. To assemble these photoetched seats run a bead of super glue along the seam lines after you bend them into shape.

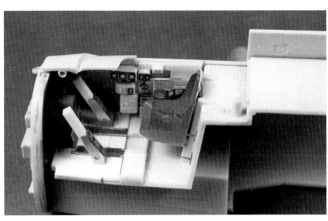

Fig. 2-61. Here the new cockpit with its interior photoetched details is getting a fit check to ensure that all the parts fit together and do not interfere with one another.

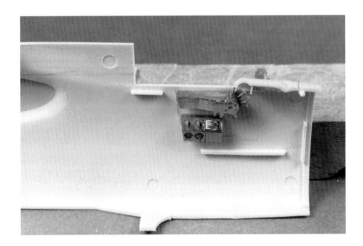

Fig. 2-62. The left side photoetched parts have also been installed and they are ready to be painted and detailed. At this point the fuselage halves are ready to be closed up with masking tape as a final fit check for all the added parts.

Fig. 2-63. The completed photoetched console has been assembled and the left surface has been drybrushed to highlight some of the surface detail. Notice how the instrument dial details stand out.

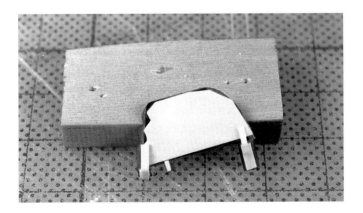

Fig. 2-64. The photoetched console's backing has a .01-inch-thick piece of sheet plastic, which serves to highlight the instrument details and strengthen the photoetch. Also note the additional strips of plastic which reinforce the photoetched switch plates.

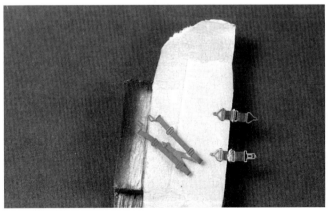

Fig. 2-65. Photoetched seatbelts take some concentration to paint because there is not a lot of relief between the belts and the harness hardware. These parts need to be carefully bent into shape so that they will fit snugly onto the seat.

Fig. 2-66. The completed photoetched seat looks good now that it has been painted and weathered and the seatbelts have been added. The seatbelts were attached with white glue.

Fig. 2-67. The cockpit interior is starting to take shape with the console, control stick, and seat added.

Fig. 2-68. The cockpit is just about complete. All that is left is to paint the left side and then glue the fuselage halves together.

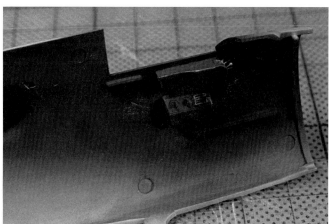

Fig. 2-69. The detail on the left side of the cockpit was picked out by drybrushing and by painting the lever handles different colors.

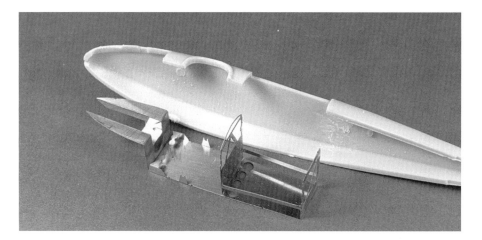

Fig. 2-70. Eduard's 1/48 scale multimedia aircraft kits also contain a lot of photoetched parts. While they are easy to build up you need to check the fit of all the parts as you proceed with the buildup of the kit. Minor adjustments to the photoetch are usually necessary to get them to fit correctly. Model by Bill Teehan.

Fig. 2-71. The completed photoetch interior and the white-metal engine on Eduard's 1/48 scale multimedia Albatross C-III are ready to install into the fuselage. Note how all the individual parts have been carefully painted. Sometimes you will also get a wavy appearance to the photoetch on long thin lengths. There is not a whole lot you can do about this type of problem, but in this case it will not really be noticeable once the fuselage is closed up. Model by Bill Teehan.

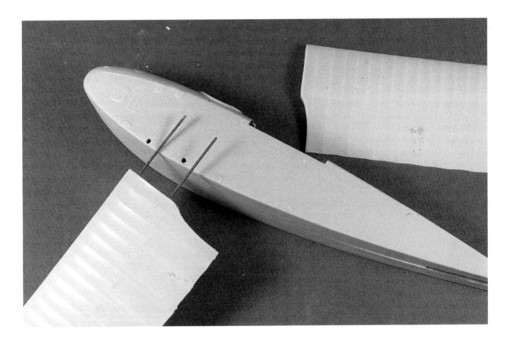

Fig. 2-72. Some resin multimedia kits do not have good attachment points for the wings so you need to make them. Two lengths of stiff brass wire are all you need to fix these problems. Model by Bill Teehan.

RESCRIBING PANEL LINES

Some model aircraft just call out for a rescribing job. This is especially true of older kits such as Revell's 1/32 scale series. While these age-old kits are accurate in shape and outline, their surfaces are covered with rivets and raised panel lines that are just out of scale. For any kit that is 1/32 scale or smaller you may want to consider sanding off the raised rivets, as they would not really be visible in these scales. Besides, if you are dealing with fit problems and have to do a lot of filling and sanding to remove the seams, the surface detail will get damaged no matter how careful you are. So, the next best step is to just sand off the surface detail and then rescribe the lines. The technique is easy and once you get some experience under your belt you will have

wild urges to do it to every kit that has raised panel lines. The tools that you will need include various grades of waterproof sandpaper, a Bare Metal Foil plastic scriber, photoetched panel scriber and shape templates, a set of sewing needles, a pin vise, Duro's white tube super glue for fixing mistakes, Scotch 3M painter's masking tape, several grade 0000 steel wool pads, and several rolls of labeling tape from a dymo labeling tape machine. You will also need some large sheets of paper for drawing the outline of the wing and fuselage halves, a ruler, and a set of dividers for measuring distances between lines. While there are several different plastic scribers available, I recommend that you invest in Bare Metal Foil's plastic scriber. It is, with-

out question, the best scriber available.

Before you sand off the surface detail you need to record the locations of the panel lines. The easy way to do this is to lay the fuselage halves and the wing halves onto a piece of drawing paper, draw their outlines, and also mark the points on the edges of the outline where the panel lines end. Since all aircraft have identical panel lines on both sides you will only need to draw the panel lines on one drawing, but remember to locate the shapes such as squares and circles on both sides. Wings can be done the same way except that you will need one upper and one lower wing drawing. After you have drawn the outlines and marked the points along the outline's edge, remove the part and then use the points along the edge of the drawing to connect the panel lines that run from one edge to another. Then use the part to measure and draw any other lines and shapes such as boxes and circles. Once this is completed you are ready to sand off the surface detail. I recommend that you do this before you assemble the kit and glue the halves together because this is a messy job that is going to put sanding dust everywhere. Use 280-rough grit to remove the detail and then go over the surface again with the same grit, but this time use water to wet-sand it. This will help smooth out the plastic. Now smooth the surface with higher grades of sandpaper by wet-sanding again. A small note here: if there is any surface detail that you do not want to remove or detail you want to protect, cover it with masking tape. Once the plastic is smooth wash it and let it dry.

Before you begin building the model, I recommend that you scribe any shapes into the fuselage and wing halves such as boxes, ovals, and circles using your photoetched scribing templates. It is easier to scribe these small shapes before the halves are glued together. In order to ensure that the shapes that you scribe are positioned correctly you will need to draw some reference lines on the surface of the part so that you can line up the template correctly. When using a photoetched scribing template you will need to use a sharp needle tip in a pin vise. It is also important to secure the template in place with masking tape once you have the shape you want to scribe positioned correctly. Be sure that the needle is secured in the pin vise tightly and that only a fraction of the needle's length is protruding from the pin vise. What you are trying to prevent is the needle flexing as you try to scribe the outline. If it does flex, the needle tip will not follow the outline of the shape on the template smoothly. Hold the pin vise at approximately a 45 degree angle and start with a very light pass and then add a little more pressure as you begin to etch into the plastic. If the needle is sharp, the etched plastic will be of sufficient depth after three or four passes. Practice makes

perfect, so do dry runs on sheet plastic first. You'll get the feel for the shape and how the needle works.

Once you have finished with the templates, assemble the model. After you have glued the halves together and completed all the seam work you are ready to begin scribing panel lines. Let's use the fuselage as an example. Using the drawing that you made as a guide for locations, pick a line that goes all the way around the fuselage. You need to set this line carefully, because all other lines on the fuselage's surface will be measured from this line once it is drawn. Measure the first line from a known point such as the front or back of the cockpit using dividers, and mark the points all around the fuselage. Then run a double thick length of masking tape around the fuselage following the marks. Next draw the line along the edge of the masking tape, remove the tape, and then check the line. You will need to make sure the line is correct in both the vertical and horizontal planes. If it's not, erase the line, make corrections to its location, and redraw it. To set additional lines around the circumference of the fuselage, use the dividers to measure the locations of these additional lines using the first line as a reference. Another method is to cut lengths of masking tape to the spacing width that you need and then run these around the circumference of the fuselage, using the first line that you drew as your reference point. Once you have all the lines that run around the circumference of the fuselage you can add the partial lines and the horizontal lines. Always remember that picking a reference point and then working from that reference point is almost a foolproof way of drawing all the vertical and horizontal lines that you need. The wings are done the same way.

Once you have drawn all the lines you are ready to apply the labeling tape and begin scribing. To increase the flexibility of labeling tape to conform to curves, cut it into thin strips. To keep the thin strips of labeling tape from moving while you are scribing a line, place wider sections of labeling tape on top of the thinner

one. Lay the straight edge of the labeling tape along the line you want to scribe and then run the scriber along the edge of the labeling tape. Hold the scriber at about a 45 degree angle and apply gentle pressure. Sometimes the scriber will move away from the edge of the labeling tape, so you will need to provide tight control without applying too much pressure. Curved surfaces take more concentration than flat surfaces and the scriber will definitely have a tendency to move away from the edge of the labeling tape along curved surfaces. If this happens, stop scribing the line. Lift the tape from the area around the mistake, apply a small drop of Duro's white tube super glue with a small wire applicator on the surface, let it dry, and sand it smooth. Then reapply the labeling tape and finish scribing. I like to fix mistakes as they occur so that I do not have to completely reapply the labeling tape along the entire edge of the line. Fuselage and wings are done pretty much the same way. For 1/32 scale kits scribe the line no more than three times, for 1/48 scale no more than two times; 1/72 scale kits would get one light pass. Scribe the lines on the wings and tail surfaces before you attach them to the fuselage. Next attach the wings and tail surfaces, fix the seams, and finish scribing any lines around these locations. You may also have to repair lines that may get damaged when you fixed the seams between the wings and fuselage. When you rescribe sections of lines to repair them, be sure that the labeling tape is set correctly along the edge of the line.

Once you have finished scribing all the lines, sand the surface using 400-grit paper or rub the surface with grade 0000 steel wool. The sanding dust will highlight the scribed lines, allowing you to check them and ensuring that you have not missed any. When you are satisfied, wet-sand the surface with 400- and then 600-grit sandpaper, and then carefully wash the surface using a soft toothbrush, liquid soap, and lukewarm water. Let the surface dry and then wipe it with Polly S plastic prep to remove any water residue.

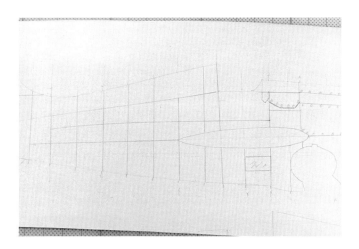

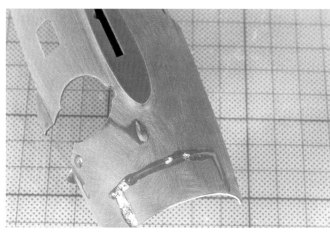

Fig. 3-1. The first step in rescribing panel lines is to draw the part so that you have a record of where the lines go. Simply lay the part on drawing paper, trace the outline, and then mark the point on the outline where panel lines end. Remove the part, connect the lines, and add additional vertical and horizontal lines and shapes.

Fig. 3-2. Super glue is the best filler for surface parts that are to be attached to the fuselage. Once the glue is dry and sanded smooth you can scribe it just like plastic.

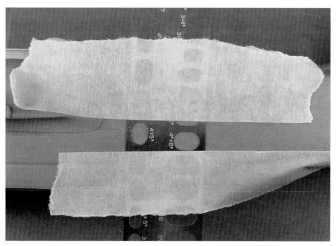

Fig. 3-3. Here is a good comparison between two fuselage halves. All the surface detail has been removed from the lower one and the plastic has been sanded smooth. The outline at the forward end of the lower fuselage is the seam where the engine inspections cover was glued in place using super glue.

Fig. 3-4. When using a scribing template be sure it is secured in place so that it doesn't move. Masking tape works best to hold scribing templates in place.

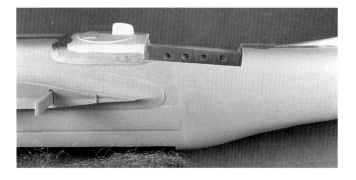

Fig. 3-5. Use 0000 grade steel wool to smooth the surface around the scribed shape. This grade of steel wool works great in combination with fine grades of sandpaper.

Fig. 3-6. It's easier to scribe small shapes with a scribing template by doing it prior to gluing the fuselage halves together.

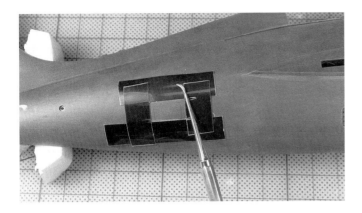

Fig. 3-7. Labeling tape can also be used when you do not have a template shape that is the right size. When using labeling tape to make shapes you can use a plastic scriber to make the panel lines. Bare Metal Foil's plastic scriber is the best product available to scribe panel lines.

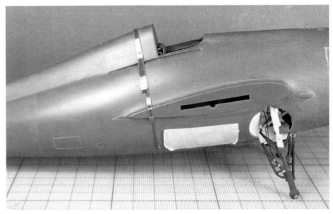

Fig. 3-8. Here the first line around the fuselage has been set. The rear wall of the cockpit was used as the location point to measure the distance from that point to the first line. Cutting labeling tape into thin lengths will allow the tape to conform to the curves of the fuselage.

Fig. 3-9. Dividers are a good tool to use to set the distance between panel lines. Once you get the distance set all you need to do is lay the labeling tape along the pencil marks. The secret is to have pencil marks all the way around the fuselage and have them spaced close together so that it will be easy to lay the labeling tape on top of them.

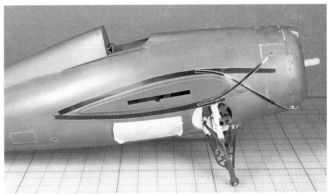

Fig. 3-10. Sometimes you just cannot cut labeling tape thin enough to get it to conform to tight curves. In these cases use sections of labeling tape positioned so that the edge the scriber will follow will be smooth and continuous.

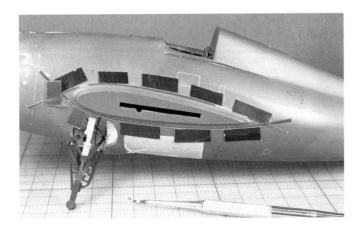

Fig. 3-11. To keep these thin lengths of labeling tape from moving when you use a scriber, back the labeling tape lengths up with thicker layers spaced close together.

Fig. 3-12. If you make a mistake scribing lines or shapes, simply apply some Duro's white tube super glue with a thin wire applicator to the area. Let it dry, sand it smooth, and try again.

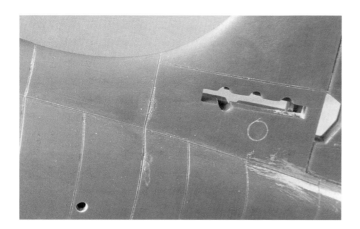

Fig. 3-13. The plastic scriber took a wrong turn along this line, but fixing it was easy with some super glue. To prevent the super glue from traveling along the scribed line when you apply it, let the glue puddle set for a few minutes before you apply some with your thin wire applicator. The glue will be slightly tacky and will not exhibit its normal capillary characteristics.

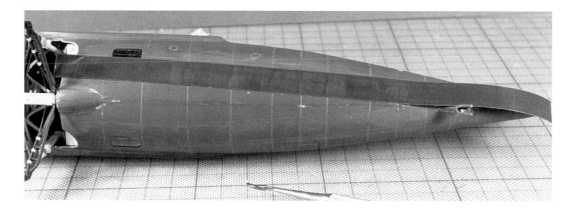

Fig. 3-14. Continuous panel lines along the length of the fuselage are easy to scribe with labeling tape. Just be careful with the scriber as you pass over an already scribed area, as the tip of the scriber will want to follow the path of the other scribed lines.

Fig. 3-15. Here the surface of the fuselage of Revell's 1/32 scale F4F Wildcat has been sanded. The sanding dust which has settled into the scribed panel lines gives you a good visual check of the location of the panel lines.

(Chapter 3 continued on page 65)

AIRCRAFT GALLERY

F4F-3 Wildcat manufactured by Revell, Inc. (1/32 scale kit built by Mike Ashey)

JU-88G manufactured by DML, Inc. (1/48 scale kit built by Scott Weller)

Boeing F4B-4 manufactured by Hasegawa, Inc. (1/32 scale kit built by John Ficklen)

Hawker Hurricane manufactured by Monogram, Inc. (1/48 scale kit built by Major Billy Crisler, USAF)

P-47D Thunderbolt manufactured by Revell, Inc. (1/32 scale kit built by John Ficklen)

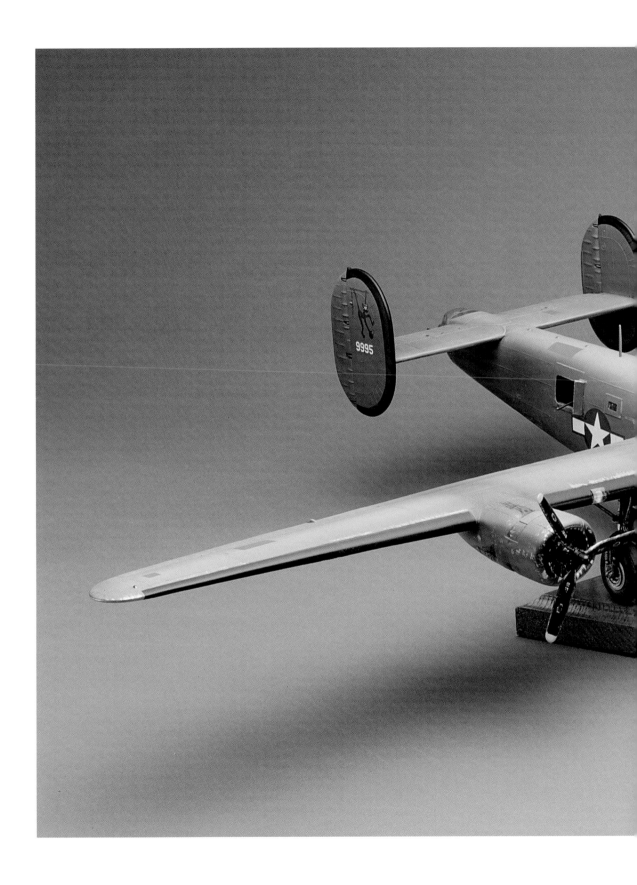

B-24J Liberator manufactured by Monogram, Inc. (1/48 scale kit built by Richard Boutin, Sr.)

Heinkel He-111 Zwilling manufactured by Italeri, Inc. (1/72 scale kit built by Scott Weller)

F9F Panther manufactured by Monogram, Inc. (1/48 scale kit built by Major Bill Crisler, USAF)

P-51 Mustang manufactured by Accurate Miniatures, Inc. (1/48 scale kit built by Richard Boutin, Sr.)

A-26B Invader manufactured by Monogram/Revell, Inc. (1/48 scale kit built by Richard Boutin, Sr.)

Albatross C. III Multi-media kit manufactured by Eduard Models, Inc. (1/48 scale kit built by Bill Teehan)

A-20G "Havoc" manufactured by Amt/Ertl, Inc. (1/48 scale kit built by Mike Ashey)

A-1H Skyraider manufactured by Monogram/Revell, Inc. (1/48 scale kit built by Mike Ashey)

F-117 Stealth Fighter manufactured by Monogram, Inc. (1/48 scale Promodeler kit built by Glenn Johnson)

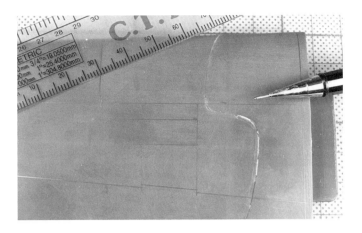

Fig. 3-16. The first step in scribing outlines for multiple box-shaped access panels is to draw the shapes on the wing.

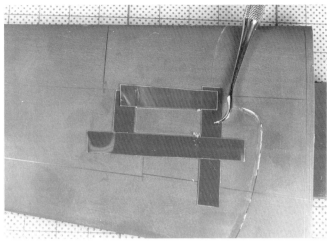

Fig. 3-17. The second step is to box in one shape with labeling tape and scribe it.

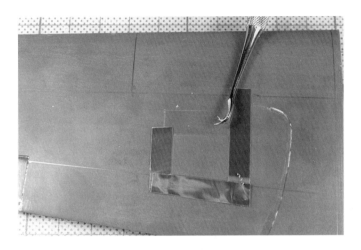

Fig. 3-18. The next step is to remove the labeling tape from the first shape, add more tape along the additional lines, and then scribe them. You need to be very careful when doing this because you do not want to run the scriber past the end points of a previously scribed line.

Fig. 3-19. Labeling tape also works great for replacing details such as the outlines of wing flaps. Here the outline of the flaps for this F4F will be scribed. To give a visual difference between the panel lines and the outline of the flaps, the flaps' lines will be scribed slightly deeper.

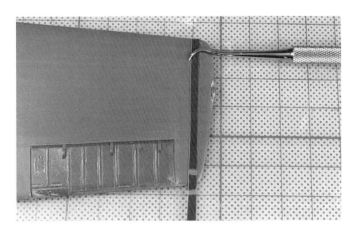

Fig. 3-20. When scribing panel lines for wings do not forget to set a scribed line at the outer edge of the wing. You need to be careful when setting the labeling tape for this line because of the compound curve areas at the tip of the wing.

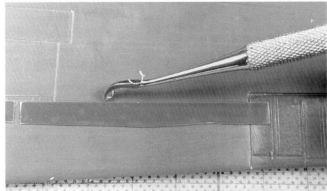

Fig. 3-21. Hold Bare Metal Foil's plastic scriber at approximately a 45 degree angle to get the best performance from this simple tool. If you hold it too high or too low it will bind with the plastic. The scriber will actually remove a sliver of plastic.

Fig. 3-22. Here the completed left wing of Revell's F4F Wildcat has been scribed, including the gun access panel. The next step will be to attach the wing to the fuselage, fix the seam and then repair any damage to the scribed panel lines that may have been caused by removing seams between the fuselage and the wing.

Fig. 3-23. An F4U Corsair has a much more complicated access panel area on its upper wings, but if you take your time and use labeling tape carefully, even these complex-looking shapes are easy to scribe.

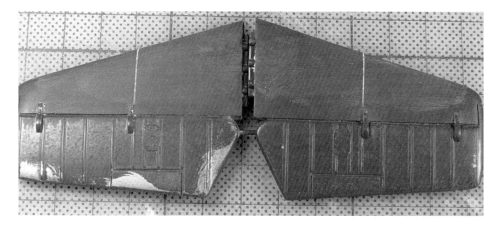

Fig. 3-24. Most elevators and rudder surfaces also had panel lines, so do not forget to add them.

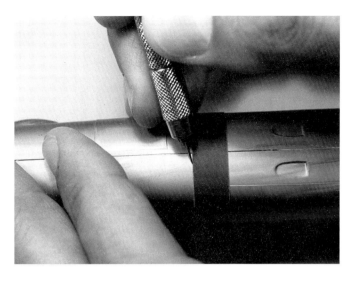

Fig. 3-25. To fix raised panel lines that have been lost because of fixing a seam, position labeling tape along the raised panel line, and lightly scribe in the line that was removed so that you connect the raised panel line to the scribed line. For these types of fixes I recommend using a needle and a pin vise.

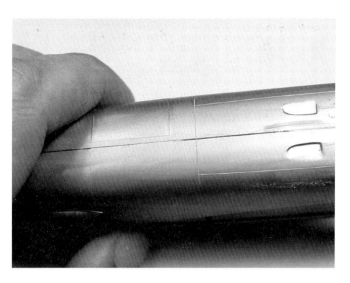

Fig. 3-26. Here the finished scribed line has been carefully sanded, and it connects very well with the raised panel lines. Once the model is painted, you will not be able to tell the difference.

Fig. 3-27. Sometimes no matter how thin you cut labeling tape, the curves are just too sharp to bend the tape around. In this case, just repair the line up to the seam point and then repeat the process for the other side.

Fig. 3-28. The scribed panel line around the trailing edge of this part has been completely restored by scribing one-half of each side at a time and connecting the scribed lines along the seam line.

Fig. 3-29. The thickness of the needle that you use will define the angle at which you have to hold your scribing tool. This is very much a trial and error process and I recommend that you experiment on sheet plastic to determine the correct angle to hold the scriber before you scribe the line.

4

ENGINE, LANDING GEAR, WHEEL WELL, AND ORDNANCE DETAILING

Engine detailing, such as adding push rods and wiring, when combined with a good paint job, can really enhance the appearance of an engine. While these details are easy to add they do take some time and prior planning. New push rods can be made from small lengths of brass or plastic rod, and wiring harnesses can be made from a combination of brass beading wire or stretched sprue. To make those molded-on details really stand out, use Testor's metalizer paints. I recommend that you drill the holes into the cylinders for the wires before you finish painting the engine. Once you have drilled the holes, paint the engine the appropriate colors and then give it a good coat of polyurethane gloss. Next apply

Testor's buffing metalizer paints using a paintbrush. The buffing metalizer paint is very thin and it will seep between all the cylinder head cooling rings while not covering the tips. This will give the engine a very nice overall multicolored appearance.

Adding brake lines to landing gear, as well as flattened tires and a good paint job, can really make these parts look good. Brake lines can be made from stiff brass wire, beading wire, or stretched sprue. To attach the brake lines to the landing gear use tiny strips of masking tape. Most brake lines were attached with flexible clamps and the masking tape simulates this very well. Flattened tires can be achieved with after-market resin tires or by flattening the bottom

of the kit's tires slightly with an iron. To get the right flatness to the tires I recommend that you flatten them with the iron after the landing gear have been glued into place. Simply hold the iron at the edge of your workbench and then place each tire onto the iron with a piece of waxed paper between the iron and the tire. The waxed paper will prevent the plastic from sticking to the iron. Watch the bottom of the tire very carefully because the plastic will start to soften and then flatten pretty quickly. Some kits have plastic located between the spoked areas of the wheel rims, and removing that plastic using drill bits and micro files will make the tires look a whole lot better. Another minor detail to add is to paint the landing gear's oleos a bright silver color. The oleo is the landing gear's shock absorber. Adding other small details such as tension springs like those found on an F4U Corsair add more realism to your model. Landing gear tension springs can easily be made by using thin copper wire lengths from household multistrand electrical wire or brass beading wire, which you wind around a small diameter length of stiff wire. Just trim it to length and attach it with super glue. If the landing gear has locking framework around the oleo that is a solid piece on the kit part, simply drill out the excess plastic and then shape the part.

Wheel wells can be greatly improved by adding framing, wiring and plumbing. Just adding a few lengths of Evergreen strip stock to give the wheel well a three dimensional appearance can make a lot of difference. If you decide to add framing or ribbing, be sure to draw the locations first so that you can lay the strips in place correctly. Plumbing can be added using lengths of stiff brass wire and interior wiring can be made from stretched sprue or brass beading wire. Even if the interior of the wheel well

was nothing more than a canvas-covered opening, as the P-40 Warhawk's were, simulating even the canvas with aluminum foil can make an otherwise bland-looking opening come alive. Scratchbuilding wheel wells is not hard to do. Like all scratchbuilding projects it takes time, but the results are often worth the effort. Whenever I scratchbuild I try to use as much of the existing kit's parts as possible so that the amount of work I have to put into a particular project will be reduced. Landing gear doors are another area where a few simple additions can make a difference. Check your documentation and add framing and inner panels to the these parts. The trick is to be sure that the framing and panels are the same on identical left and right wing doors. You can also add the hinges for these doors using your Waldron punch or by just adding actuator arms.

Ordnance like guns and bombs can also be detailed. The best detail you can add to guns is to drill out the openings of the gun's tips so that they appear hollow. On fighter aircraft drill out the shell ejection ports and do not forget to add those gunpowder smoke trails across the upper and

lower surfaces of the wings. If the gun's tips are too small to drill out, replace them with small brass tubing. Even 1/72 scale diameter brass tubing can be found in hobby stores that carry HO and N scale model railroading supplies. Ordnance can be dressed up by adding the fusing wires and adding instruction type decals to simulate the actual instruction stencils that were imprinted on the sides of bombs and rockets. On 1/48 and 1/32 scale kits you can also add the disks that are located on the tips of the bomb rack clamps using your Waldron punch tool. Drop tank brackets also had these small disks attached to their tips. When attaching bombs and rockets be sure that they are straight and level and that they are all in line. This is especially important with multiple rocket launch brackets on WWII and Korean aircraft, where you could have in excess of six rockets under each wing. Painting bombs and rockets cannot be overlooked, and if you take the time to add yellow stripes on bombs and paint rocket tips red with mid-body stripes of green or olive drab, you can really enhance the appearance of these parts.

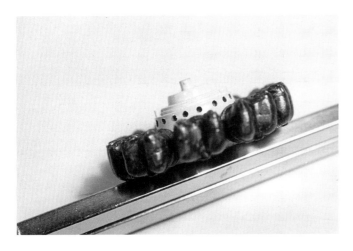

Fig. 4-1. To add push rod detail to radial engines, the first step is to drill holes around the perimeter of the engine part to accept plastic rod. Set the spacing using a pair of dividers.

Fig. 4-2. The push rods on the left engine were individually cut, sprayed with Testor's metalizer, and then form-fit into place.

Fig. 4-3. The wiring harness on this engine part was made by wrapping a thin strip of Evergreen strip stock around its base. The individual wire rings were made with a Waldron punch tool.

Fig. 4-4. Once the individual disks were glued in place the centers were drilled out to accept the wires.

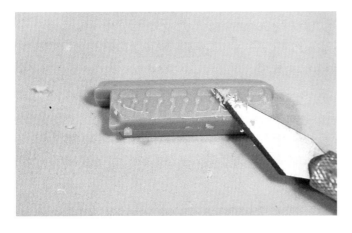

Fig. 4-5. Some kit-supplied engines need to have molded-on detail scraped off before you can add new detail.

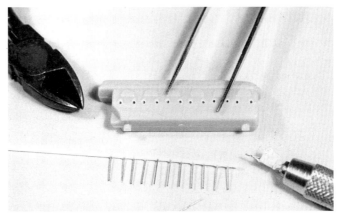

Fig. 4-6. The individual spark plug holes for this in-line engine were drilled out. To simulate the wiring harness, small lengths of brass wire were glued to a length of Evergreen rod.

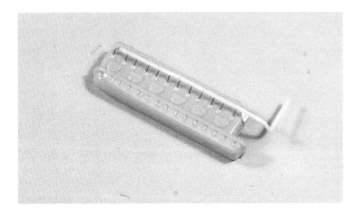

Fig. 4-7. The wiring harness brass wire lengths were cut to size and pushed into the drilled holes and then the Evergreen tubing was bent to shape. The addition of simple details like this can greatly enhance the appearance of any engine.

Fig. 4-8. In order to add wiring details to this engine, corresponding holes were drilled into the engine cylinders as well as around the rim of the engine case.

Fig. 4-9. The next step is to paint the engine. Here the background disk for this engine part has been painted interior green and the cylinder heads masked.

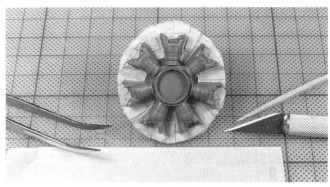

Fig. 4-10. Now the background disk has been masked and the engine cylinders will be painted light gloss gray.

Fig. 4-11. Both of these engine parts have now been painted the base colors and they are ready for painting the individual cylinders.

Fig. 4-12. The individual cylinders were painted with a small flat brush using Testor's buffing metalizer paints. The buffing metalizer paints are much thinner; when applied with a brush the paint will seep in between the ridges of the individual cylinders, resulting in a nice two-tone effect. This only works when applying the metalizer paints to a gloss surface.

Fig. 4-13. The individual brass wire lengths are cut and form-fit into place and then secured with Elmer's glue. Even though the individual brass wire lengths were pre-painted, the form-fitting process usually scrapes some of the paint off, resulting in some touch-up work.

Fig. 4-15. Here the photoetched wiring harnesses have been added, and in combination with good painting these engines look much more realistic.

Fig. 4-17. A combination of wiring, surface detail, and painting on this 1/32 scale P47 have resulted in a very realistic engine. Model by John Ficklen. Photo by Glenn Johnson.

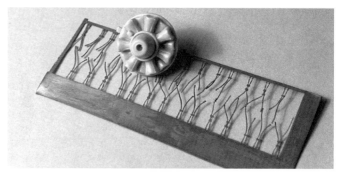

Fig. 4-14. Photoetched wiring harnesses can greatly enhance the appearance of engines that do not have much surface detail.

Fig. 4-16. The small lengths of wire added to the engines of Monogram's 1/48 scale B-25 greatly enhanced the overall appearance of the model.

Fig. 4-18. Wiring and plumbing galore adorn the interior engine compartment and machine gun bay of this 1/32 scale Hasegawa FW-190. Model by John Ficklen.

Fig. 4-19. Even if you have no plans to add wiring or other details, a good paint job in combination with weathering will help enhance an aircraft engine. The sooty effect on this aircraft engine was achieved with pastel dust.

Fig. 4-20. Sometimes jet engine aircraft have intakes with flaws or seams that are hard to fix. As an alternative, make an intake cover plug, which all jet aircraft have, and insert it into the intake to hide the flaws. Photo by Glenn Johnson.

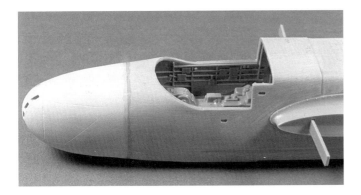

Fig. 4-21. To replace simulated screening with real screening for engine intakes, the first step is to remove the plastic. By drilling multiple holes into the surface you will greatly facilitate the removal of the plastic.

Fig. 4-22. The next step is to use the tip of a no. 11 X-acto blade and cut the plastic between the drilled holes.

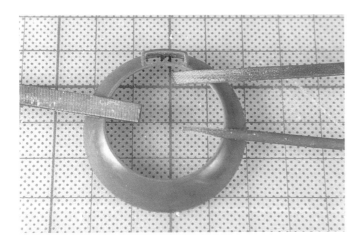

Fig. 4-23. To remove the remaining plastic, shape the opening and thin the edges using micro files.

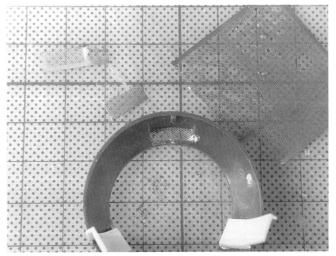

Fig. 4-24. Cut the screening to shape, insert it into the opening for the backside of the part, and glue it into place with a small amount of super glue.

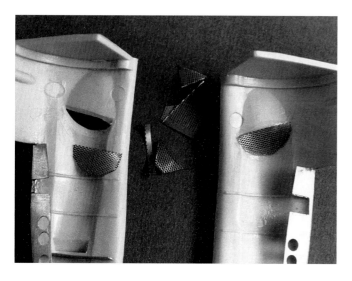

Fig. 4-25. To enhance the appearance of the air intakes on AMT's A-20G Havoc, screening was cut to shape and then glued into place on the back side of the openings.

Fig. 4-26. To improve the appearance of large air intakes, such as the ones found on Revell's 1/32 scale F4F Wildcat aircraft, remove the molded-on air intakes. Such large molded-on detail can be removed by slowly peeling away the plastic with a no. 11 X-acto knife and then sanding the surface flat.

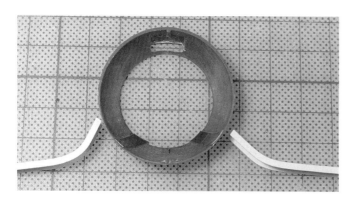

Fig. 4-27. To make new air intakes for this F4F, Evergreen channel stock was used. The plastic was softened by placing it against a 100-watt light bulb and then pushing against the interior cone shape of the cowling to shape it. The edges of the labeling tape acted as a locating lip for these parts as they were being form-fit into place.

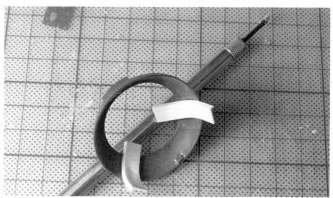

Fig. 4-28. Here the new air intakes have been glued into place. The excess length made it easy to install them and once the glue is dry they will be cut to the correct length.

Fig. 4-29. Here the finished air intakes have been trimmed to size.

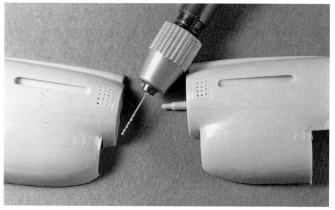

Fig. 4-30. The appearance of the engine breather holes on this 1/72 scale P-40 were greatly enhanced by drilling out the individual holes. This is yet another example of how a simple modification can greatly enhance the realistic appearance of any scale model.

Fig. 4-31. The molded-on air outlets for this 1/32 scale F4U Corsair were removed with Bare Metal Foil's plastic scriber. The openings were then shaped with micro files.

Fig. 4-32. To scratchbuild a new vent opening, simply tape some plastic sheeting to the inside area of the opening and draw the outline onto the sheeting.

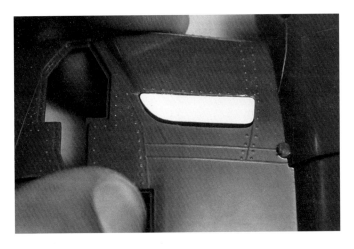

Fig. 4-33. Here the new part was cut from the plastic sheeting, shaped, and installed. This air outlet opening is more realistic in its appearance.

Fig. 4-34. Drilling out the exhaust ports is another simple enhancement that you can make. These exhaust ports are being drilled out using a Dremel drill press, although they could have just as easily been drilled out by hand.

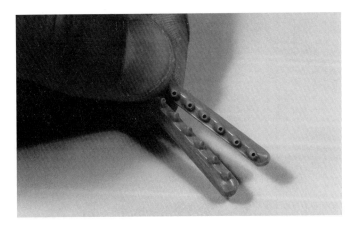

Fig. 4-35. Hollowing out engine exhaust ports on kit-supplied parts makes a big difference in their overall appearance.

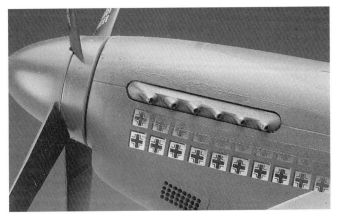

Fig. 4-36. The combination of drilled-out breather holes, drilled-out exhaust ports, and exhaust stains and weathering on the nose area of this P-51 Mustang makes for a very realistic scale model. Photo by Glenn Johnson.

Fig. 4-37. Sometimes just deepening the exhaust ports can greatly enhance their appearance. These 1/48 scale A-20G Havoc exhaust ports will look a lot better once the inside areas are painted black and the cowlings are installed.

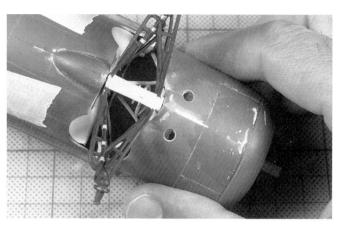

Fig. 4-38. Sometimes kit-supplied exhaust ports just beg to be replaced. This is especially true of exhaust ports that are molded onto the fuselage, as on Revell's F4F Wildcat. Here the molded-on exhaust ports have been drilled out.

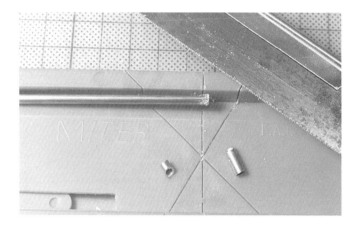

Fig. 4-39. New exhaust ports can be replaced with either brass or plastic tubing. The exhaust ports for this Revell F4F are being scratchbuilt from brass tubing and cut with a miter box and a razor saw.

Fig. 4-40. Check the angles of the new exhaust ports to ensure that they follow the contour of the fuselage.

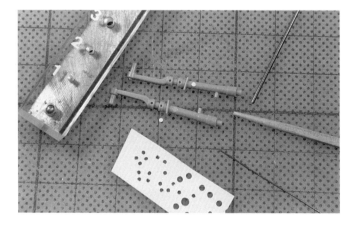

Fig. 4-41. Landing gear are notorious for having punch-out indentations, but these are easily fixed with a Waldron punch tool, some thin sheet stock, and a drop of super glue.

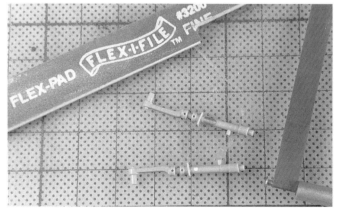

Fig. 4-42. To smooth out the small plastic disks and to remove the seam lines along the sides of the landing gear, scrape the seam lines flat using a no. 11 X-acto blade and then use a Flex-I-File sanding stick and sander to contour the shapes of the landing gear.

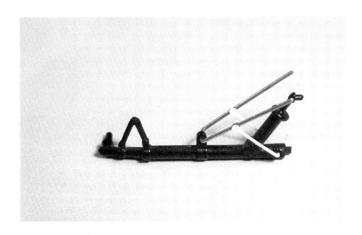

Fig. 4-43. Some landing gear like this 1/32 scale example need additional details. The bent brass rod will also add to the strength of the landing gear.

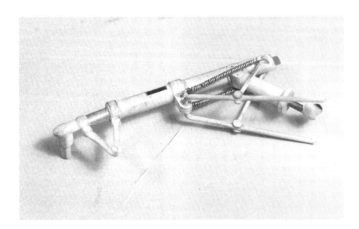

Fig. 4-45. The springs were cut to length and then glued to the landing gear after it was painted and weathered.

Fig. 4-47. The leaf spring on this 1/48 scale landing gear should not be a solid piece, but that can easily be fixed. The first step is to draw the outline of the area of plastic that will be removed.

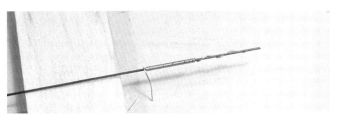

Fig. 4-44. Many different types of landing gear have large springs as part of the gear mechanisms, and these are easy to duplicate with soft brass beading wire wrapped around a stiff length of wire.

Fig. 4-46. The final product looks great once it is installed; and combined with landing gear wheel well and door details, the overall appearance can be dramatic.

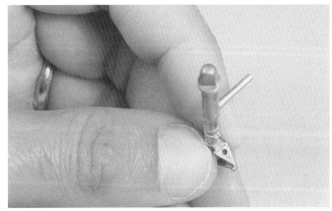

Fig. 4-48. Next, drill a series of holes inside the area to be removed so that you can work the tip of a no. 11 X-acto blade into the holes to remove the remaining plastic.

77

Fig. 4-49. The last step is to use a micro file to shape the area. Now the landing gear has a much more accurate-looking leaf spring.

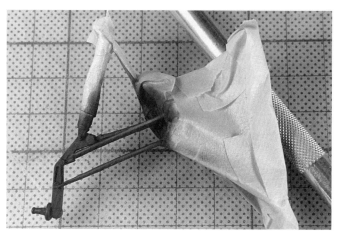

Fig. 4-50. Some landing gear assemblies were multicolored, and when the landing gear is as complex as an F4F Wildcat's was, the masking can be a bit tricky. The secret is to mask one side at a time and use small strips to build up the masked area.

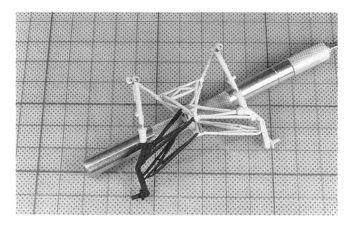

Fig. 4-51. Now one side is complete and the other side will be masked and painted.

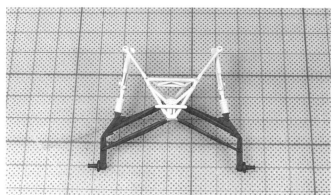

Fig. 4-52. The painted two-color landing gear looks great and it's all because of careful masking. Also note the silver color applied to the oleos.

Fig. 4-53. Do not forget to add details to the rear landing gear. Springs, cables, and extra parts make this landing gear almost a model in itself. Model by John Ficklen. Photo by Glenn Johnson.

Fig. 4-54. Hydraulic brake lines are easy to add with some stretched sprue or brass wire. Some lines were made from flexible hoses and others were made from tubing, so be sure to check your documentation.

Fig. 4-56. The landing gear on this P-47 look great with brake lines. Model by John Ficklen. Photo by Glenn Johnson.

Fig. 4-55. Thin strips of masking tape simulate the clamps that are usually used to attach the brake lines to the landing gear. And when painted silver, they help enhance the appearance of the landing gear. Photo by Glenn Johnson.

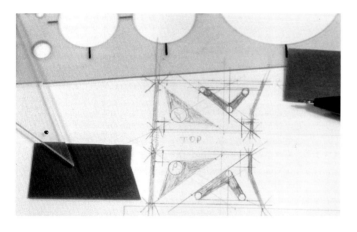

Fig. 4-57. The first step in detailing landing gear doors is to draw the parts that you need to make.

Fig. 4-58. Landing gear doors are usually too thick. To thin them, tape them to a length of balsa wood and then run the part across a stationary piece of sandpaper. Be sure that the sticky side of the tape is covered.

Fig. 4-59. The interior plastic on these landing gear doors was cut out and then glued into place.

Fig. 4-60. Circular hinges can be made by using two different size Waldron punches and then cutting the resulting doughnut-shaped disks.

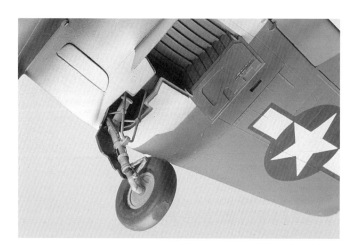

Fig. 4-61. Once the doors have been painted and weathered and the hinges have been added, they really enhance the appearance of this F4U's landing gear wheel well. Photo by Glenn Johnson.

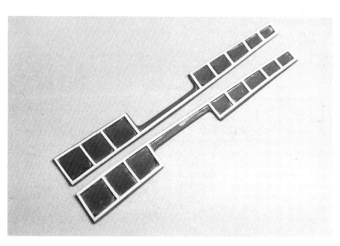

Fig. 4-62. Framing can easily be added to the inside of landing gear doors, but the secret to getting both sides to look the same is to draw lines where the strip stock will go and then carefully glue them into place.

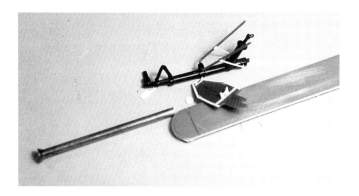

Fig. 4-63. Support framing for wheel well doors that attach to the landing gear can also be made by punching a hole into a length of sheet stock and then cutting around the hole to get the correct shape for the support frame.

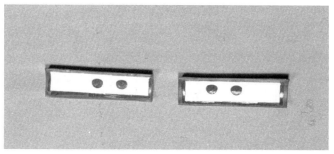

Fig. 4-64. Just adding small lengths of sheet stock with holes punched in them to the inside area of an otherwise bland-looking surface can enhance its appearance. To get the inner sheeting to conform to the curved surface of the door, the sheeting was pressed against the door using a small wood dowel of the same diameter and then glued into place.

Fig. 4-65. Even on 1/72 scale kits, if you add nothing more than some sheet stock with holes punched into it you will improve the appearance of a wheel well.

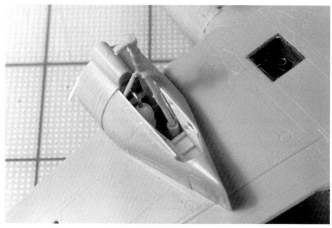

Fig. 4-66. This 1/72 scale kit not only has sheet stock, but also has added framing, cylinders, and tubing. Model by Scott Weller.

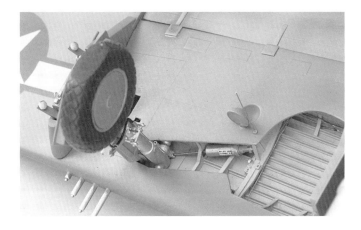

Fig. 4-67. 1/32 scale models have always been perfect for adding a lot of detail to a landing gear area that is readily visible to the eye, and this P-47 is no exception. Model by John Ficklen. Photo by Glenn Johnson.

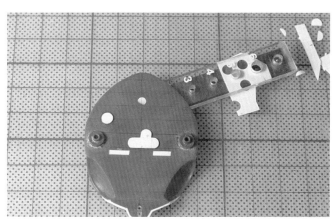

Fig. 4-68. The first step in detailing the firewall on Revell's 1/32 scale F4F Wildcat is to begin adding the chain drive disks. Here is another good example of using Waldron's punch tool to scratch-build parts.

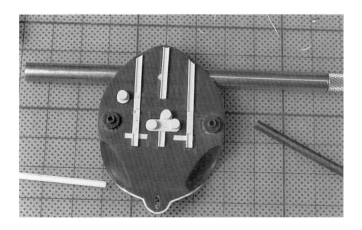

Fig. 4-69. Here the chain drive disks are complete, and small lengths of Evergreen channel stock have been modified and then attached to the firewall. Also note the small strip of plastic added to the bottom of the firewall to fix a spacing problem.

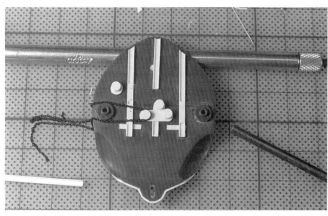

Fig. 4-70. Next, the three individual lengths of chain must be measured and cut. The chain, which is HO scale model railroad detailing hardware, can easily be found in well-stocked hobby stores.

Fig. 4-71. The finished scratchbuilt firewall details get one last fit check with the landing gear to ensure that everything looks good.

Fig. 4-72. Here the firewall has been installed and painted and the chain has been added. The chain really enhances the interior area of the landing gear bay, besides providing a high level of accuracy.

Fig. 4-73. Even adding small lengths of bent brass wire and photoetched plumbing can enhance a wheel well. The photoetched part came from Teknics 1/48 scale landing gear plumbing set.

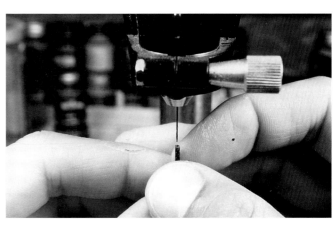

Fig. 4-74. Hollowing out the tips of machine gun barrels can easily be done using a Dremel drill press.

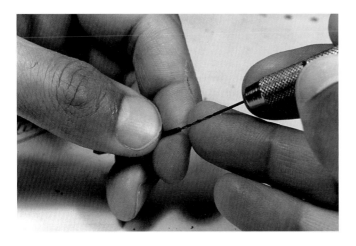

Fig. 4-75. You can also hollow out large-scale guns by hand using a pin vise.

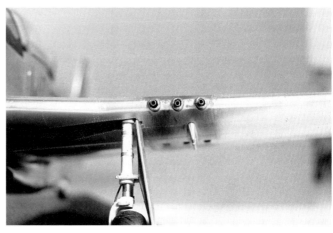

Fig. 4-76. The kit supplied machine guns on this P-51 Mustang were hollowed out with a pin vise. To get the edges thin, the tip of a no. 11 X-acto blade was slowly rotated around the hole to peel away the plastic.

Fig. 4-77. WWI machine guns can be enhanced by using photoetched parts in combination with kit-supplied parts.

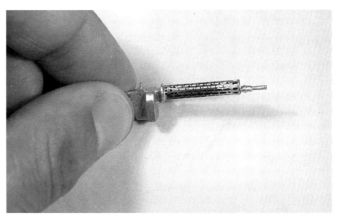

Fig. 4-78. Here the photoetched parts have been assembled and silver paint has been used to check for any cracks and flaws.

Fig. 4-79. The machine guns on this WWI triplane have been painted with Testor's gun metal and polished with a Q-tip. The combination of these photoetched parts and the kit's parts is a real eye-catcher.

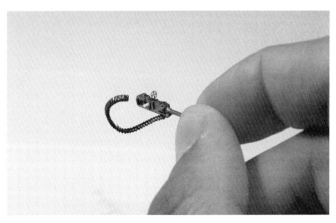

Fig. 4-80. This 1/48 scale waist gun for a 1/48 scale B-25 has been enhanced with a photoetched gunsight ring, a slightly larger charging handle made from plastic rod, and a machine gun belt cannibalized from a 1/48 scale Monogram Huey.

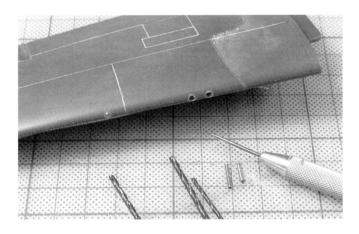

Fig. 4-81. The first step in installing brass or stainless steel tubing in wings to simulate machine gun barrels is to drill oversize holes in the leading edges of the wings.

Fig. 4-82. Here the two brass rod lengths are being checked to ensure that they seat correctly in the holes.

Fig. 4-83. The nose guns on Monogram's 1/48 scale Panther were replaced with stainless steel tubing. This is another good example of how adding these types of minor details can enhance the appearance of a model. Model by Maj. Billy Crisler. Photo by Glenn Johnson.

Fig. 4-84. Don't forget to drill out machine gun shell ejection ports. And the best way to remove the plastic is to start by using a drill bit.

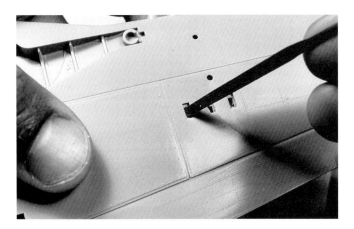

Fig. 4-85. Once you have removed the excess plastic from the ejection port opening using the tip of a no. 11 X-acto blade, shape the opening with micro files.

Fig. 4-86. It's easier to separate the bomb casing from the fin before you attempt to remove the parts from their pour plugs.

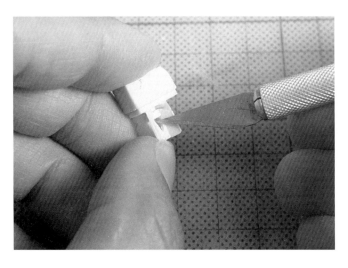

Fig. 4-87. Before you remove the bomb's fin from the pour plug remove the excess flash from the fin's framing using the tip of a no. 11 X-acto blade.

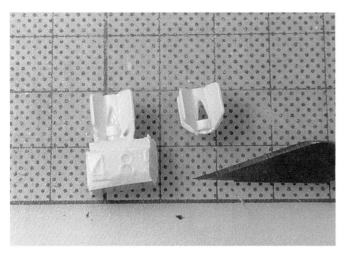

Fig. 4-88. Once the flash is removed from the fin you can separate the fin from its pour plug.

Fig. 4-89. To flatten the surfaces where the pour plugs were located, carefully run the base of the fin and the base of the bombshell across a piece of stationary sandpaper.

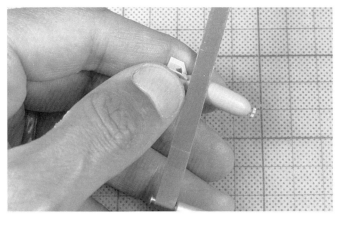

Fig. 4-90. Flex-I-Files work great to contour the connection point between the bombshell casing and the fin, and also to smooth the surface of the bomb.

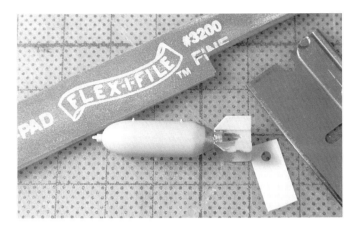

Fig. 4-91. Because the resin fins are so thin they will occasionally break off, but the fix is easy. Just take a small piece of sheet stock, cut it to shape, and glue the new fin in place.

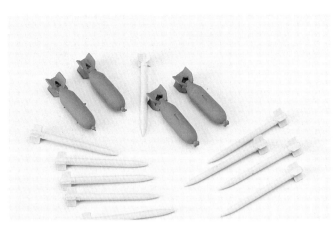

Fig. 4-92. Assemble all the ordnance such as bombs and rockets that you plan to use on an aircraft, clean them up, and paint their base colors all at the same time. Photo by Glenn Johnson.

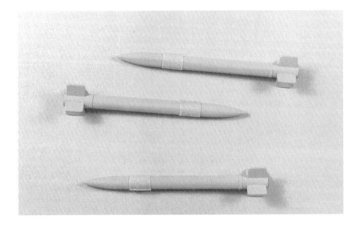

Fig. 4-93. Rockets usually have colored tips and then stripes along the body. Simple masking with thin strips of masking tape is all you need to make these multicolor parts. Here the outlines of the rockets' painted tips have been masked and the remaining body of the rocket will be covered with a larger piece of masking tape.

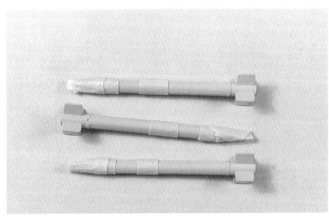

Fig. 4-94. Once the tips have been painted, mask them over and begin locating the stripes.

Fig. 4-95. Don't forget to add the yellow stripes on bombs, which is easy to achieve with masking tape.

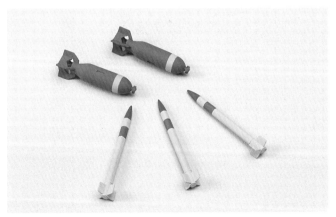

Fig. 4-96. These bombs and rockets have been painted and they're ready for the next step. Photo by Glenn Johnson.

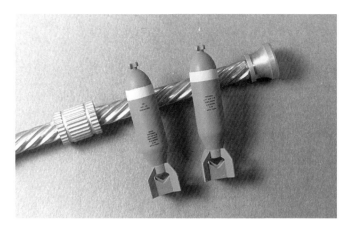

Fig. 4-97. Bombs usually have instruction stencils on them, so don't forget to add this small detail.

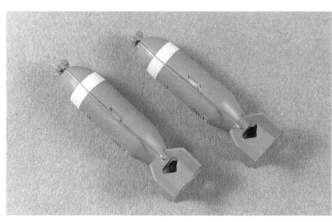

Fig. 4-98. Bombs also have fusing wires and this detail is easy to add using small lengths of brass beading wire.

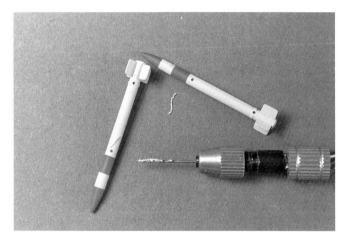

Fig. 4-99. Individual rocket parts usually need to have their locating pin holes slightly deeper so the rockets will sit on the pedestals correctly.

Fig. 4-100. Be sure that your rockets are parallel to the wing and to each other. Photo by Glenn Johnson.

Fig. 4-101. The combination of bombs, rockets, and four potent 50-caliber machine guns packs a heavy punch. Photo by Glenn Johnson.

Fig. 4-102. Another good example of bombs and rockets with different base and stripe colors. Also note the instruction decals on the pylons. Model by Maj. Billy Crisler. Photo by Glenn Johnson.

Fig. 4-103. If you decide not to add ordnance but to retain the pylons, be sure to add detail to these parts. Model by John Ficklen. Photo by Glenn Johnson.

5

CONTROL SURFACE DETAILING

The overall appearance of aircraft models can be greatly improved by repositioning the control surfaces. This is especially valuable if you are creating any type of diorama. Aircraft are seldom seen with all their control surfaces in neutral positions with flaps retracted. There are several different approaches to repositioning control surfaces that you can take. The first one is to carefully cut out the control surfaces and flaps, fill in the voids, make new hinges, and then reattach them. The second approach is the same as the first except you use two kits. One is the finished kit and one is the sacrifice kit. Sometimes it is almost impossible to cut out the control surfaces and flaps on some aircraft kits without damaging the cut-out parts. Using this second approach you can cut out the control surfaces from one model without worrying about damaging the control surfaces and flaps, and then cut around the control surfaces and flaps on the second kit without worrying about the surrounding wing surfaces. Then all you need to do is mate the wings from the first model to the control surfaces and flaps of the second model, fill in the voids on these parts, make new hinges, and reattach them. The third approach is to cut out the control surfaces and flaps without worrying about damaging them and replace them with aftermarket ones made from resin. Most of the resin detail sets for control surfaces are in 1/48 and 1/72 scale, and companies like KMC and Aeromaster, as well as several others, produce excellent parts that are easy to use. I do suggest that you make sure you can get a set of resin control surfaces before you start hacking away at the kit's wings.

The secret to cutting out control surfaces and flaps is to glue the wing sections together and use a Bare Metal Foil plastic scriber to cut through the engraved channels around a control surface and the flaps that form the outline of the parts. Other tools that can be of assistance in cutting out control surfaces and flaps are a razor saw, a jeweler's saw, and a plastic scriber. If you do not have a plastic scriber, use a sewing needle and a pin vise. If you are working with control surface outlines that are raised instead of engraved you will need to secure some type of guide along the edge where you want to cut. The same type of labeling tape that you use to scribe panel lines works great for setting the outlines and providing an edge to guide your cutting tools. When using a razor saw be careful that you do not cut too far into the plastic. A jeweler's saw will have a tendency to migrate away from a cutting line because the saw blade is so thin—so be careful.

When cutting out the parts, cut through one side and then turn the wing over and cut through the other side. Sometimes there can be a slight difference in the locations of the engraved lines and if you cut all the way through from one side, you may end up cutting into the wing. How the hinges are set on the control surfaces will dictate whether you fill the voids created by removing the part first or cut out the hinge locations and then fill in the voids. You can fill the voids with a variety of materials including Evergreen strip and sheet stock, thick gel super glue, and resin. You may also find that combinations of these materials may be beneficial, depending on the shape of the control surface and the void areas in the wing. You also need to be careful when filling these voids, especially in the wing, so that you do not change the shape of the wing. The best way to avoid this is to carefully set small spacers between the inner area of the wings first and then fill in the area between the spacers.

The big difference between working with control surfaces and flaps is that you may also need to add detail to the flaps as well as the interior of the wing area depending on what type of aircraft you are working with and also how the flaps work. Some flaps just rotate while others both extend and rotate at the same time. As an example, a B-17's flaps rotate down, exposing the interior of the trailing edge of the wing and the underside of the flap. In this case you would need to add wing rib and stringer detail to the underside of the wing and reinforcing framing to the underside of the flap. Other types of aircraft, like a P-51, have flaps that just rotate a section of the trailing edge of the wing. This is the simplest type of flap to reposition. The flaps on an F4U Corsair, on the other hand, have sections of the trailing edge of the wing that rotate as well as extend, exposing the interior of the wing. When adding this type of interior detail, reference material and drawings are important. If you do not have any, add some details like wing sections and stringers if the interior of the wing is exposed.

When repositioning the control surfaces, be sure that the ailerons are set in opposite positions and that the angle between the wing surface and the ailerons is the same. Typically, ailerons have a slight upward and downward position when aircraft are parked. Rudders do not usually move very far from left to right so be careful how far you reset them. Elevators need to be set at the same angles, either up or down, and typically they are set downward. This is so that if a strong wind hits the aircraft from the front or back the aircraft will be pushed down by the position of the elevators. Flaps can be set to any angle, but typically the angle is not much except when the aircraft is ready to take off. Be sure that the flaps are all set at the same angle and position and that all flaps on each wing are set at the same angle and position.

Another important detail on control surfaces that modelers sometimes overlook is the positioning of the control surface tabs. These tabs are adjusted by the pilot to relieve the pressure of the control stick so that the pilot can almost take his hand off the stick. To enhance their appearance, run the plastic scriber into the channel that forms their outlines so that they will have an enhanced appearance. If there are external cables that position these tabs, add them. This is a great visual enhancement on 1/32 and 1/48 scale kits. Many World War I biplanes had external control, pulleys, and cam systems for the control surfaces, and adding these little details can really enhance the realism of these types of airplanes, especially the 1/48 and larger scales. For 1/48 scale kits use nylon sewing thread for these cables; on 1/32 and 1/28 scale kits you need a slightly thicker cable, so use stretched clear sprue. Do not use cloth sewing thread because it attracts dust and is very difficult to get taut.

Cutting out and repositioning all the control surfaces as well as adding detail to them can become overwhelming, especially if you have a lot of voids to fill, hinges to add, and clean-up work to do. Sometimes it's best to select just some control surfaces to do or just do the flaps. This is especially good advice if you have not done this type of detailing before.

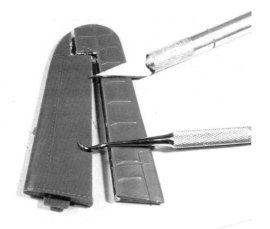

Fig. 5-1. There are several different ways to remove control surfaces; the method you use depends on the situation. In most cases using Bare Metal Foil's plastic scriber to cut most of the way through the plastic and then using a sharp no. 11 X-acto blade to cut the rest of the way through works very well.

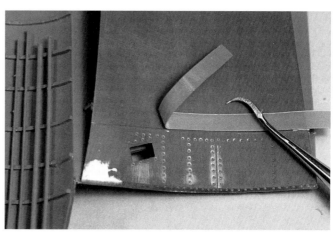

Fig. 5-2. While almost all control surfaces have engraved outlines, some models have flaps that have raised lines to define their shapes. In these cases, use labeling tape to outline the shape and then use your plastic scriber to remove the part.

Fig. 5-3. Once you have cut a deep channel in the plastic, to speed up the process you can use a razor saw to finish cutting through the plastic.

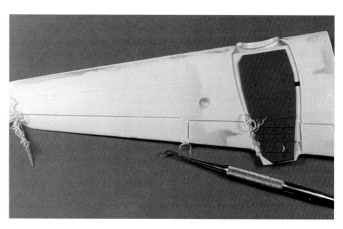

Fig. 5-4. The ailerons and flaps on AMT's 1/48 scale A-20G Havoc have been deeply cut with a Bare Metal Foil scriber. Because of the odd shape of these parts, they will have to be segmented to remove them.

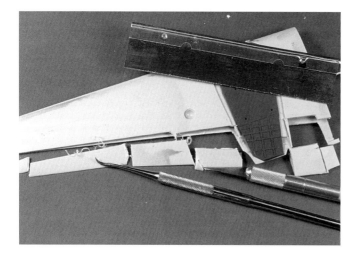

Fig. 5-5. Here the ailerons and flaps have been removed. The next step will be to clean and square the edges and thin the inside surfaces of the wing where these parts will attach. In order to remove these control surfaces, the parts were damaged. Thanks to resin manufacturers, modelers can buy ready-made control surfaces, which reduces the amount of repair work that you have to do.

Fig. 5-6. Some control surfaces are stepped and you have to use a combination of scribing tool, a razor saw, and a jeweler's saw. Here again the rudder on this part has been severely damaged, but it will be replaced with a new resin rudder.

Fig. 5-7. Removing both the ailerons and flaps on wings can make them very fragile. I recommend that you add scraps of plastic to the inside area of the wing wherever possible to reinforce it.

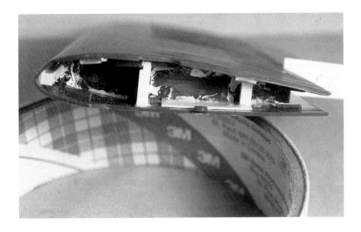

Fig. 5-8. Another good example of reinforcing the inside area of a wing. Since this wing is in two parts, you can seal off a small area inside this section of the wing. Once you glue the wing halves together, pour resin into the void, which will strengthen this two-part wing.

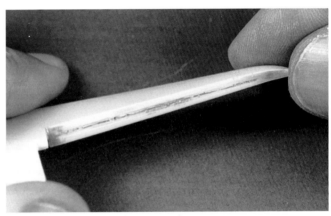

Fig. 5-9. To fill small voids that are created when you remove control surfaces such as elevators or rudders on 1/48 or 1/72 scale kits, simply fill the void with thick gel super glue and sand it smooth.

Fig. 5-10. On large-scale kits you can use thin sheet stock or a combination of sheet stock and resin to fill the large voids that are created when you remove the control surfaces.

Fig. 5-11. Here the completed tail of Revell's 1/32 scale Corsair has been sealed using sheet stock, and silver paint was used to check the seams.

Fig. 5-12. The corresponding rudder for this Corsair will be sealed using a combination of sheet stock and resin. Here oversize sheet stock was glued to the openings. Once the glue is dry, the sheet stock will be cut down and shaped.

Fig. 5-13. Here the elevator opening has been sealed on this wing surface and the excess plastic has been slowly peeled off.

Fig. 5-14. The quick way to get the edges straight is to run the part across a stationary piece of sandpaper.

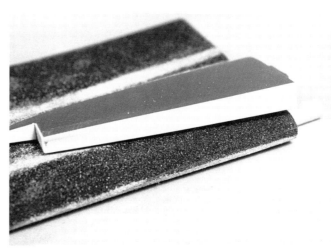

Fig. 5-15. To achieve a curved inner surface, simply run the plastic across an appropriate-sized dowel wrapped in rough-grit sandpaper.

Fig. 5-16. To facilitate filling a control surface with resin, sandwich the control surface between two strips of balsa wood so that it is level and then cover the sides with masking tape. The advantage to using resin is that it is a quicker way to fill a void area than to cover it with plastic and shape it.

Fig. 5-17. To give a control surface a rounded edge, simply run the part across a stationary piece of sandpaper and rotate the part as it moves across the surface. A nice advantage to using resin is that it shapes easily.

Fig. 5-18. Another good example of using resin to fill a control surface. Resin also adds a great amount of strength to these small parts by completely filling the cavity.

Fig. 5-20. Here thick plastic stock has been added to the inside portion of these Corsair flaps to create a longer flap. After the glue dries the parts will be cut and sanded to shape.

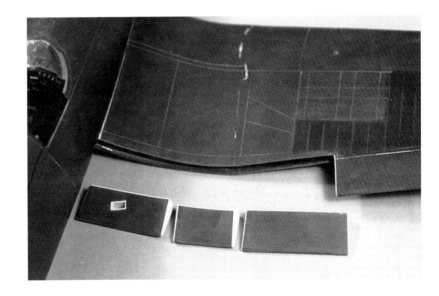

Fig. 5-19. The flaps on this 1/32 scale Corsair have been cleaned and the sides sealed. At this point they are going through their final fit checks before plastic is added to the inside area.

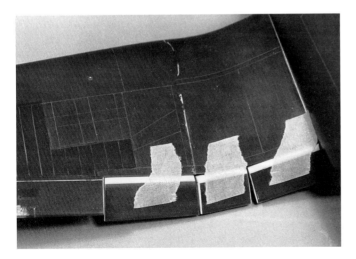

Fig. 5-21. Here the completed flaps with their added plastic are receiving their final fit check.

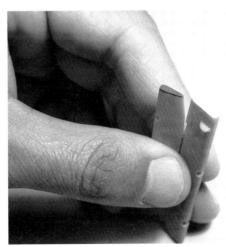

Fig. 5-22. Plastic was added to the edges of these control surfaces so that they would fit snugly into their openings. Don't forget to check for these small details.

Fig. 5-23. The tail control surfaces on Revell's 1/32 scale P-40 Warhawk were designed as separate parts but there are spacing problems. To fix these spacing problems use the same techniques of adding small strips of plastic. Photo by Glenn Johnson.

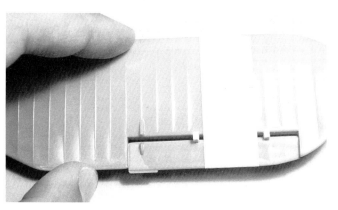

Fig. 5-24. The first step in adding hinges is to pick a strip stock size close to the hinge size that you want, install the hinges in the control surface, and tape it into place. Next apply a tiny amount of super glue to the back side of each hinge so that it is attached to the wing.

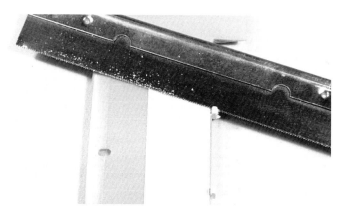

Fig. 5-25. At this point remove the control surface and run a bead of super glue around the entire perimeter of strip stock. Then cut the strip stock to size using a razor saw or sharp knife. To protect surface detail cover it with masking tape.

Fig. 5-26. Shape the hinges by wrapping a piece of sandpaper around a sanding block and rotating the sanding block around the edges of the plastic strip to give it a curved shape.

Fig. 5-27. Here a final fit check is done on the hinges to ensure that they fit correctly.

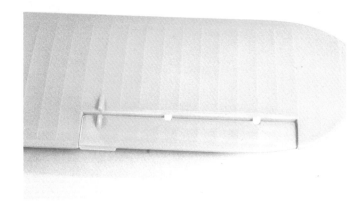

Fig. 5-28. A good example of control surfaces with multiple hinges that have been removed and reattached. Careful cutting, measuring, and shaping will always give you good results. Photo by Glenn Johnson.

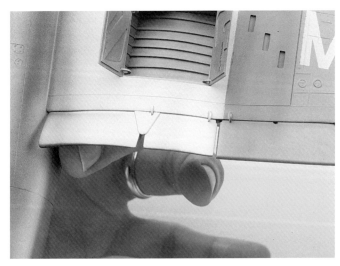

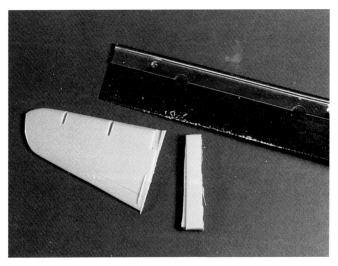

Fig. 5-29. The hinges on the flaps of this F4U Corsair were made with a Waldron punch tool. Photo by Glenn Johnson.

Fig. 5-30. The first step in working with resin control surfaces is to remove the part from its pour block. Be careful when you do this, as these parts are easily damaged.

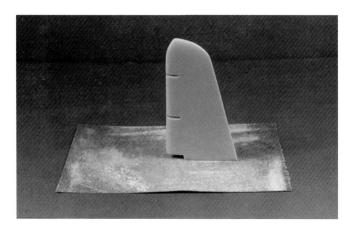

Fig. 5-31. To flatten the contact point between the control surface and the pour block, run the control surface across a stationary piece of sandpaper. You need to be extra careful to hold the part flat so that you don't end up with an angled surface.

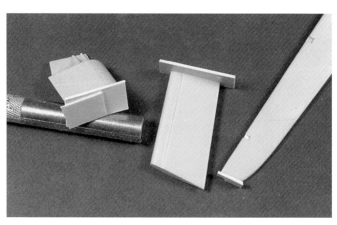

Fig. 5-32. Some resin control surface detail sets need additional plastic so they fit tightly in their openings.

Fig. 5-33. Trim the excess plastic with a sharp single edge razor blade or a no. 11 X-acto blade to remove as much of the plastic as possible. Since resin sands very easily, it's important to minimize the amount of sanding work that you have to do.

Fig. 5-34. These resin flaps and aileron are getting a final fit check to determine if they need additional plastic.

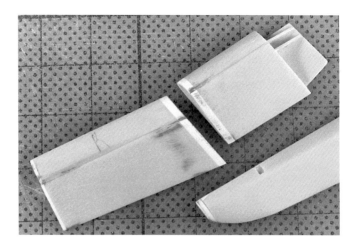

Fig. 5-35. These resin flaps and aileron are now ready to be painted and then installed into the wing. While the ends of these parts needed a significant amount of additional plastic, it was quicker than having to build up the control surfaces and flaps that were cut out of the wing.

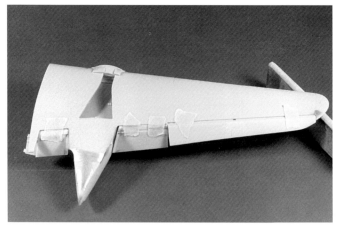

Fig. 5-36. Here the ailerons and flaps have been taped into place to ensure that enough plastic has been scraped from the inside area of the wings so that these parts will sit in place correctly.

Fig. 5-37. With control surfaces attached and clear parts masked, this A-20G is ready for painting.

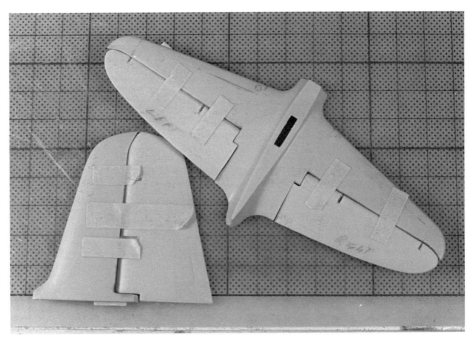

Fig. 5-38. Resin elevators and rudders are usually a lot less complicated to add, but you need to be careful not to damage the shape of these parts or the corresponding wing area as you sand and shape them.

6

PAINTING, DECALS, WEATHERING, AND SIMPLE DISPLAY BASES

There are several simple steps in painting that are an absolute must if you want to get good results. First, you have to ensure that the plastic parts are clean and free of sanding dust and residue. Give all the parts a cleaning with Polly S surface preparation cleaner.

To get a quality finish or to mix colors to get various shades and fading effects, you cannot get by without an airbrush. Since temperature and to a large degree humidity affect airbrushing, you should do all your painting in a moderate temperature and low humidity environment. Generally, temperatures between 65 and 75 degrees are good and humidity of no more than 60–65 percent is acceptable. The thinner that you use is also important, and I always use the manufacturers' recommended thinners. To get the most from each bottle of paint, drop a few copper BBs into the bottle to help mix up the sticky paint on the bottom of the bottle. Thinning paint for airbrushing can sometimes be a trial and error process, and there is also a relationship between paint thinning ratios and the air pressure you use. Generally, I use a mixture range of four parts paint to one part thinner to three parts paint to one part thinner at between 22 to 28 pounds of air pressure. I have tried a lot of different air supplies and the easiest and quietest is by far a CO_2 bottle with a pressure regulator. While the setup cost is a little more than a small compressor, the air is always dry, the air flow is consistent and adjustable, it's as quiet as a church mouse, and a bottle typically lasts me two years.

When you are ready to paint, secure the parts with masking tape on either lengths of balsa wood or stiff cardboard sections so that you will not be handling the parts. As a rule of thumb, give all parts a coat of primer first. The only time you would not use a primer is when you are using metalizer-type paints. Primer provides a good adhesion surface for paint and the primer color will also highlight any flaws, cracks, seams, and scratches that you may have missed. If you do find any areas that need additional finishing work, let the primer dry for a few days, fix the problem areas, and then sand the surrounding primer using a minimum of 600-grit sandpaper. To blend in the unpainted and primer painted areas, first give the unpainted area a coat of primer and then give the entire area a complete coat so that both the old and new primer are covered.

The finish coats of paint should not be rushed and you should let the paint dry for a least 48 hours before you handle the model or apply a second coat. Gloss paint takes longer to dry and it may be several days before a gloss paint like white really dries. As a rule of thumb, if the surface smells like fresh paint it's still drying. Once you are finished painting the next step is to add the decals.

Keeping your airbrush clean is also very important. I run thinner through the airbrush between colors as well as cleaning the tip. When I am finished with each airbrushing session I disassemble the airbrush and clean it using tissues, thinner,

and pipe cleaners. To make enamel-base paint flow more smoothly I warm the paint on a coffee warmer, always keeping the lid open a crack so that pressure will not build up. The paint only has to be on the warm side to get it to flow smoothly. If you are using spray paint let the can sit upside down for a few hours and then give it a good shaking. Spray paint can also be warmed by setting the can in hot water for a few minutes. Always test the paint before using it and clean the spray tip when you are done. To remove excess paint from the tip, hold the can upside down and spray until no paint comes out. If you are using a hand brush, add a few drops of thinner and BBs to the paint and mix well. Thinning the paint slightly will help it flow better. Paintbrush selection is also important and I use only natural hair brushes that keep their shape. Clean your brushes after every use and run them under hot water to reshape them.

The secret to decal application is to apply the decals to a gloss surface, to cut as much of the clear film from the decal as possible, and to use decal-setting solutions that make the decal snuggle up around surface details. If you used gloss paints you are ready to add the decals; if you used a flat colored paint, then you need to add a gloss finish. I have tried a lot of gloss finishes and I have had the most success with water-base clear gloss paint, although it tends to clog my airbrush. Water-base clear gloss works well on either water- or enamel-base surfaces. I have also had a lot of success using a clear gloss polyurethane paint, the kind you find in hardware or home supply stores.

Once you have glossed the surface, apply a test decal to a test surface first, unless you know for sure that the decals you are using are good decals that will respond to setting solution and will not silver. I have had problems with some manu-

facturer's decals that do not respond at all to setting solution and silver even if they are applied to a gloss surface. I always try to use after-market decals, which are designed for setting solutions, unless the kit has a set of decals that have been manufactured by an after-market decal manufacturer. Always cut the decals free from their sheets using a sharp knife and a ruler. Cut as much of the clear film off as possible. For small decals like instruction labels or serial numbers, cut around the perimeter. For large numbers or letters cut out each one individually, remove all the clear film and then apply them one at a time. The trick is to ensure that they are lined up correctly. Insignia should also have all the clear film trimmed away. For curved areas like circles use a series of tangential cuts to trim away the excess film, and for straight cuts use a metal ruler as a guide.

Cut decals one at a time and dip them in warm water with tweezers for a few seconds so that the decal absorbs the water. The decal is ready to apply when it slides off the backing. Slide the decal slightly off the backing, lay the decal on the model, and then slide the remaining portion off the backing while holding the decal in place with a moist Q-tip. The gloss surface will allow you to slide the decal around a bit to position it. If the decal starts to dry, moisten it with some water applied with a Q-tip. Let the decal dry, then apply coats of setting solution to the surface using a Q-tip. After a few coats the decal will soften and snuggle up around the raised detail and into or around panel lines. Sometimes the decal will wrinkle when you apply the setting solution. If this happens push the decal back down with a damp Q-tip. When you have finished applying all the decals, clean up the surrounding surfaces of the decals to remove any water stains and then give the decals a coat of clear gloss to protect them.

Now comes the fun part, weathering. If you are going to weather your model heavily I recommend that you lighten the surfaces of the airplane that would normally be exposed to the sun. These would be the upper surfaces of the wings and the upper area of the fuselage. The easiest way to do this is to spray a coat of highly thinned white or light gray over these surfaces using a water-base paint. How much you want to lighten the surfaces and the decals will dictate how much paint you will be mixing. Generally, I use 25 percent paint to 75 percent thinner. One light coat is all you need, as you do not want to overdo the effect. Next drybrush silver paint mixed with some black to tone down the bright silver appearance on the leading edges of the wings, tail, rudder, and any wing surfaces that would show wear due to walking. Your drybrush strokes should be from the leading edge to the trailing edge of the wing. This effect should be very subtle. Next add exhaust stains for the engine exhaust ports and gunpowder stains at the gun locations. When you have finished weathering, give the entire model a coat of clear flat.

Simple display bases will help protect your model from careless hands and allow you to view the model up close without breaking it, or marring the surface by handling it. Wood display bases cut from oak, hard rock maple, walnut, or mahogany with routed edges make excellent display bases. To secure the model to the base, drill holes in the bottoms of the tires and glue plastic rod into them. Then drill corresponding holes into the display base and then drill large holes into the bottom of the display base about ½ inch in diameter and about ⅛ inch deep into the wood. Cut plastic disks slightly smaller than the ½-inch diameter holes, and then drill holes into the center of the disks the same size as the rod that you glued into the tires. Slip the rods through the holes of the display base, making sure that the tires are sitting flat on the surface of the display base.

To secure the model, slip the cut plastic disks over the rod, glue the plastic with super glue, and then trim the excess rod. Several manufacturers also make display bases and diorama displays using resin and photoetch, and some have even designed their bases to fit AMT/ERTL's clear display covers.

Fig. 6-1. One of the last stages of preparation of a model prior to painting is to polish the surface and smooth out the plastic. There are several ways to do this. One way is to use finer grades of sandpaper up to 600 grit, and another method is to use Bare Metal Foil's liquid plastic polish.

Fig. 6-2. Revell's F4F Wildcat is assembled and once it is masked the painting process will begin. Note that the plastic surface has been sanded smooth and lightly polished. Photo by Glenn Johnson.

Fig. 6-3. Scotch 3M painter's masking tape cut into small strips works great for masking landing gear.

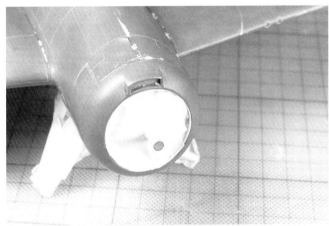

Fig. 6-4. Here combinations of small strips of masking tape and a large piece cut into a disk shape with a center hole punched cover the engine area of this F4F Wildcat very well.

Fig. 6-5. Here's another good example of using combinations of thin strips of masking tape with larger sections to cover the fuselage area of this airplane. The tail surfaces on this model are ready to be painted yellow.

Fig. 6-6. Here the Wildcat has been primed and is ready for the first application of additional masking. Once you have primed the model, check it one last time for flaws and cracks, repair those areas, and reprime. Photo by Glenn Johnson.

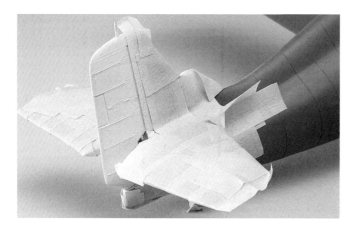

Fig. 6-7. This F4F Wildcat will have a red and white striped rudder. The first step is to paint the entire rudder white. Here again, use small strips of masking tape to cover the surface areas. Photo by Glenn Johnson.

Fig. 6-8. The next step is to cut strips of masking tape the thickness of the stripes, position them on the rudder, and spray the surface red. Photo by Glenn Johnson.

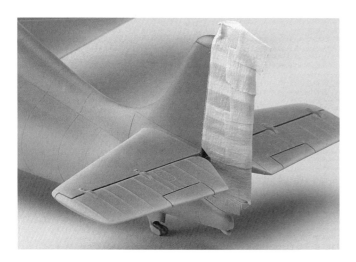

Fig. 6-9. Once the red paint is dry, remove all the masking and then completely mask the rudder. Photo by Glenn Johnson.

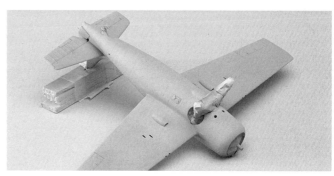

Fig. 6-10. The next step is to paint the undersurfaces of the aircraft light gray. When painting such large surface areas, remember that you do not have to coat the entire surface in one application. It's better to have several thin coats than one thick coat. Photo by Glenn Johnson.

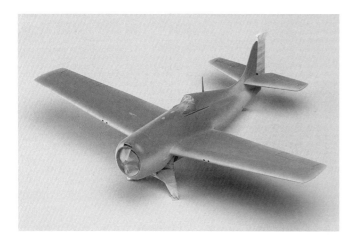

Fig. 6-11. Once the underside paint is dry, the model is flipped over and is ready for the upper color. Photo by Glenn Johnson.

Fig. 6-12. Here the upper color has been carefully applied and the entire model has been given a gloss coat. By carefully positioning the airbrush and holding the aircraft at different angles while painting the upper surface, you can get good demarcation lines along the wings and good feather lines along the fuselage. Photo by Glenn Johnson.

Fig. 6-13. One of the fundamentals of decal application, aside from applying decals to a gloss surface, is to remove as much of the carrier film as possible from the surface of the decal.

Fig. 6-14. Q-tips dampened with decal-setting solution work great for both sliding the decal from its backing and positioning it correctly.

Fig. 6-15. Applying decal-setting solution will soften the decal and allow it to conform around raised detail. This decal took seven applications of setting solution to get it to conform around the raised surfaces.

Fig. 6-16. Even small decals should have as much clear film as possible cut from around the sides of the decal to reduce the risk of silvering.

Fig. 6-17. Cut a large decal like this into smaller parts, remove all the clear film, and then position each image. This approach is a must when there's so much clear film on a decal.

Fig. 6-18. After all the decals are set, apply dulled Testor's silver paint to the leading edges of the wings and to the tail, cowling, and areas where pilots and maintenance crews walk. Photo by Glenn Johnson.

Fig. 6-19. Add the gunpowder smoke burns to the upper surfaces of the wings and also exhaust stains from behind the cowling flaps. Once you have finished weathering, paint the model with Dullcote. Photo by Glenn Johnson.

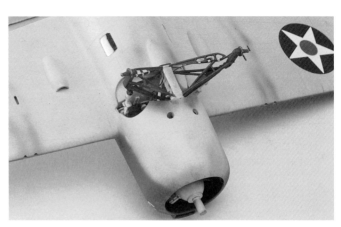

Fig. 6-20. Don't forget to apply gunpowder stains to the underside of the wings and behind the machine gun shell ejection ports, and to apply exhaust stains for the mufflers. Photo by Glenn Johnson.

Fig. 6-21. Don't forget to weather the inside of your model. The sooty, dirty effect on this 1/48 scale A-26 was achieved using Tamiya's smoke X-19 colored paint. Model by Richard Boutin, Sr. Photo by Glenn Johnson.

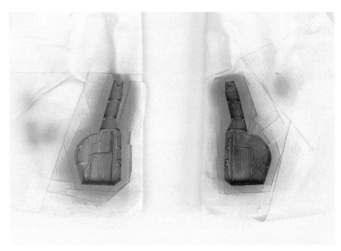

Fig. 6-22. The left wing wheel well has received its final application of pastel dust, while the right one has just been drybrushed with silver paint. Photo by Glenn Johnson.

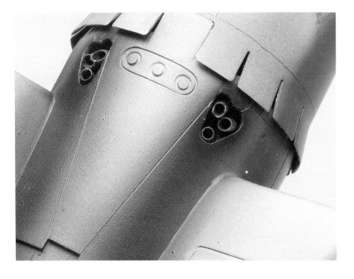

Fig. 6-23. The exhaust stains on this F4U Corsair were achieved using a combination of Testor's dark metalizer paints and flat black applied as separate coats. Sometimes the application of heavy exhaust stains can also help to hide minor flaws. Photo by Glenn Johnson.

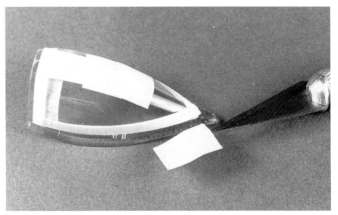

Fig. 6-24. Scotch 3M painter's masking tape also works great for masking clear parts. For this canopy, long thin strips of tape were cut and positioned along the edge of the framing to box in the area that needed to be masked.

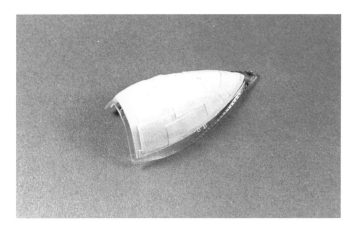

Fig. 6-25. Here the completed upper surface of the canopy is ready to be painted.

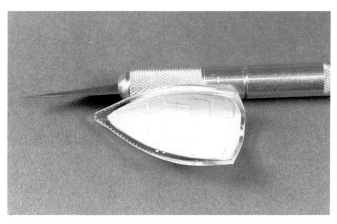

Fig. 6-26. When masking canopies, don't forget to cover the underside. Since the inside of canopies do not have any framing you need to mask the outer surface first, and then use the locations of the masking tape as a guide to placing the tape on the underside.

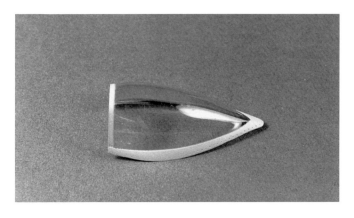

Fig. 6-27. Here the completed canopy is ready to be attached to the model. The secret to ensuring that you get sharp painted edges is to burnish the masking tape down with the tip of a pencil.

Fig. 6-28. A trick for painting canopies with criss-crossed framing is to mask the canopy framing in one direction and paint it.

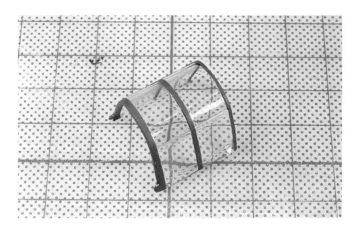

Fig. 6-29. Here the canopy framing has been painted from left to right and is now ready for the second application of masking tape.

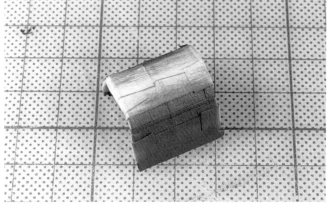

Fig. 6-30. Here the canopy framing from front to back has been masked and painted. Be sure to let the paint dry at least 48 hours prior to applying masking tape to it.

Fig. 6-31. The rear canopy on this F4F Wildcat was painted using this stepped approach and the results are sharp and well defined. Photo by Glenn Johnson.

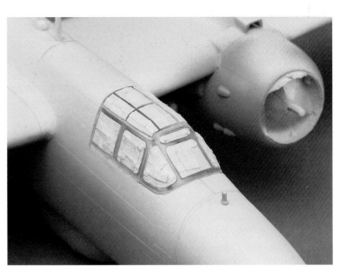

Fig. 6-32. Another good example of canopy masking. Here the canopy was glued into place first, then masked.

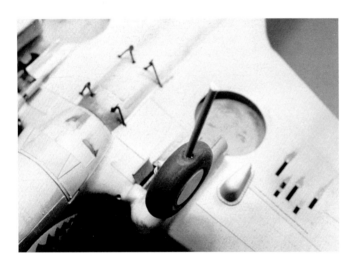

Fig. 6-33. To positively secure a model to a wood display base, drill small holes in the bottoms of the tires and glue pieces of plastic rods into the holes.

Fig. 6-34. Don't forget to drill a hole in the tail wheel as well and attach a piece of rod to it. If the model is displayed at an angle, you do not want it to tip off the display base because the rear wheel was not secured.

Fig. 6-35. To mark the location of the holes on a wood display base, position the model on the base and then mark the points where the plastic rods are resting. Once the locations are marked, drill holes all the way through the wood display base the same diameter as the rod. The next step is to turn the display base upside down and with a drill enlarge the holes about a third of the way up through the bottom.

Fig. 6-36. Complete staining the base, and then cut plastic disks slightly smaller than the hole's diameter. Drill holes in the center of the disks the same size as the diameter of the rod. Next position the model on the display base, slide the rods through the holes in the wood, slip the disks over the rods, glue in place, and cut the excess rod. The model is now secured to the base. Photo by Glenn Johnson.

Fig. 6-37. Routing the edges on the display base in combination with selecting a stain color that complements the surface color of the model adds to the overall effect of your finished masterpiece. Photo by Glenn Johnson.

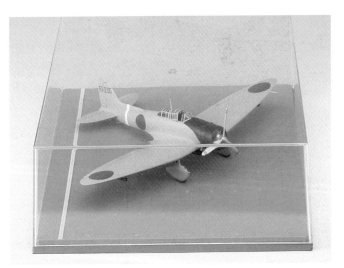

Fig. 6-38. Cottage industry companies such as Classic Warships produce simple display bases that also double as diorama bases. Their carrier deck display bases add a nice presentation effect to 1/48 scale naval aircraft and these display bases are also designed to accept AMT/ERTL's large display case. Photo by Glenn Johnson.

Fig. 6-39. This impressive 1/200 scale simple diorama by Glenn Johnson is mounted to a wood display base. The B2 Bomber and KC 110 Tanker are suspended by a thick stainless steel wire embedded in the refueling probe. The KC 110 Tanker is manufactured by Hasegawa and the B2 Bomber is manufactured by DML. Photo by Glenn Johnson.

Fig. 6-40. Eduard's 1/48 scale Albatross C-III sitting on top of Rockford Boulder Company's diorama display base. Model by Bill Teehan.

SUPPLIERS AND MANUFACTURERS

AeroMaster/KMC
3615 N.W. 20th Ave.
Miami, FL 33142
(Resin detail sets, paints, decals)

Badger Airbrush
9128 West Belmont Ave.
Franklin Park, IL 60131
(Airbrush equipment)

Bare Metal Foil Company
P.O. Box 82
Farmington, MI 48332
(Plastic polish, plastic scriber, decals, resin, RTV rubber)

Borden Inc.
Department CP
Columbus, OH 43215
(White glue)

Carrier Deck Accessories (Classic Warships)
P.O. Box 57591
Tucson, AZ 85732
(Photoetched detail sets, resin dioramas, carrier decks)

Creations Unlimited Hobby Products
2939 Montreat Dr. N.E.
Grand Rapids, MI 49509
(Flex-I-File and Flex-I-File sanding sticks)

Cutting Edge/Meteor Productions
P.O. Box 3956
Merrifield, VA 22116
(Resin detail sets)

Devcon Corporation
Danvers, MA 01923
(Two-part epoxy)

Dremel
4915 21st St.
Racine, WI 53401-9989
(Drill bits, cutters, drill press, motor tools, drill press vise)

Eduard M.A. Ltd.
P.O. Box 17A
434 Olmost
Czech Republic
(Multi-media kits, photoetched detail sets)

Evergreen Scale Models
12808 N.E. 125th Way
Kirkland, WA 98034
(Plastic strips, rod, sheeting)

Floquil-Polly S
206 Milvan Dr.
Weston, ON M9L 1Z9
Canada
(Paints, plastic prep and paint/decal remover)

K & S Engineering Co.
6917 59th St.
Chicago, IL 60638
(Sandpaper, brass rod and tube)

Loctite Corporation
4450 Cranwood Ct.
Cleveland, OH 44128
(Super glue)

Micro Mark
340 Snyder Ave.
Berkeley Heights, NJ 07922-1595
(Hobby supplier)

Microscale Industries, Inc.
1570 Sunland Lane
Costa Mesa, CA 91710
(Decal setting solution, decals)

Model Technologies
13472 Fifth St., Suite 12
Chino, CA 91710
(Photoetched parts)

Northwest Short Line
P.O. Box 423
Seattle, WA 98111
(Chopper and true sander)

Pacer Technology
9420 Santa Anita Ave.
Rancho Cucamonga, CA 91730
(Super glue accelerator)

Plastruct
1020 South Wallace Place
City of Industry, CA 91748
(Plastic shapes and rod)

Reheat Models
1A Oak Drive
North Bradley
Trowbridge
Wiltshire, BA14 OSW
England
(Photoetched detail sets, instrument decals)

Rockford Boulder Company
869 Kingsway Road
Tallahassee, FL 32301
(Specializing in display bases using sand, soil, and rock from around the world)

Scotch 3M Painters Masking Tape
P.O. Box 33053
St. Paul, MN 55133
(Masking tape)

Small Parts Inc.
13980 N.W. 58th Ct.
P.O. Box 4650
Miami Lakes, FL 33014
(Steel wire and hollow wire)

Squadron Shop
1115 Crowley Dr.
Carrollton, TX 75011
(Modeling accessories, detail sets)

Super Scale International, Inc.
2211 Mouton Dr.
Carson City, NV 89706-0471
(Decals, decal-setting solutions, and white glue)

Teknics
13472 5th St. Suite
Chino, CA 91710
(Photoetched and resin detail sets, resin engines)

Testor Corporation
620 Buckbee St.
Rockford, IL 61104-4891
(Paints, paintbrushes, putty, sandpaper, glue and glue applicators, sprue cutters, airbrush equipment)

True Details
P.O. Box 115010
Carrollton, TX 75011
(Resin cockpits, wheel detail sets)

Verlinden Productions
Lone Star Industrial Park
811 Lone Star Dr.
O'Fallon, MO 63366
(Resin and photoetched accessories and detail sets)

Waldron Model Products
P.O. Box 431
Merlin, OR 97532
(Waldron punch set, placards, instruments, and photoetched parts)

X-Acto
230 S. Broad St.
Philadelphia, PA 19102
(Blades and cutting tools)

INDEX